Congo's Post-Traumatic Legacy of King Leopold II

Irenee KAYEMBE MBOMBO

Congo's Post-Traumatic Legacy
of King Leopold II
Irenee kayembe Mbombo

Design ©Tricorn Books
www.tricornbooks.co.uk
Text & Images ©E Sommers

ISBN 978-1-909660-85-4
Published 2017 by Tricorn Books
28 Landport Terrace, Portsmouth PO1 2RG

Printed and bound by CPI Group (UK) Ltd, Croydon, CR0 4YY

Dear Michael,

I hope you get inspired by
reading this book as I was
inspired by researching it. !
For little Nathan !

KAYEMBE

Congo's Post-Traumatic Legacy
of King Leopold II

This book is dedicated to the memory to my
parents Meta and Kalonji Swing Baleka,
who provided me with love, toil and the
foundation to mould, build and shape the
person that I have become.
To my children Meta, Bijanu, Ndaya and
Tshibangu. May this book contribute to
enrich your knowledge, give you an insight of the
history of your origin so that you
become aware of your value, to contribute to the
development of your personality
and the creation of your own reality.
To my wife Marie-France Kayembe, for all the
love, the care and even the
harassment that made me get back
down to earth

Acknowledgement

I would like to say my gratitude to my sisters and brothers, who stood by me, guided and supported me in writing this book. I could not have made it through without particularly the encouragement and faith in my work by Topaze Kayembe, Ndaya Therese, Marius Baloji and Jean – Claude Kalambay. I thank Barbara O'Sullivan my oldest and dearest friend, for her inspiration and support. She has always been there as a moral compass through different stages of my expedition. There are many more people, friends and families I could thank, but time, space, and modesty compel me to stop here.

Contents

Introduction

As Carter G. Woodson once put it *"If you can control a man's thinking you do not have to worry about his action. When you determine what a man shall think you do not have to concern yourself about what he will do. If you make a man feel that he is inferior, you do not have to compel him to accept an inferior status, for he will seek it himself. If you make a man think that he is justly an outcast, you do not have to order him to the back door. He will go without being told; and if there is no back door, his very nature will demand one."*

As soon as I started paying close attention to things going on around me and around the world, I decided to use my mind as a parachute; this has to be opened, for it to work. I was born in a black country where the majority of people were black. I grew up developing, like all young people of my generation, a sense of trust or sympathy toward the few European folks who crossed my path, such as teachers -the development of a positive feeling and admiration for the structures and systems put in place by the colonial system.

When I finished my primary school located in my catchment area, I moved to a school in the town centre, around 10 miles away from home. The only European I knew, before I got to this new school, was our parish priest from Belgium. In my new school, there were European teachers, all of them from Belgium. They were living in a convent of Xaverian Brothers. The Xaverian Brothers or Congregation of St. Francis Xavier (CFX) was a religious institute founded by Theodore James Ryken in Bruges, Belgium in 1839 and named after Saint Francis Xavier. The institute was dedicated to Roman Catholic education, working alongside the missionary priests.

I became so anchored in the positivity of the entire colonial education system that when I went to university to study Economics Sciences, I decided to undertake another course about human rights with the United Nations Office for Human Rights on the 50th anniversary of the Declaration of Human Rights. At no time during my study journey, in any history book or support material was anything mentioned in relation to the Congo history of human rights abuses.

I knew almost nothing about Congo colonisation until when I was 20 years old and at the university. Then, I read a book "Du sang sur les lianes: Leopold II et son Congo" by Daniel Vangroenweghe. Although the account in the book was particularly striking, it didn't occur to me to question deeply what had happened; instead, I wondered why it was that the country couldn't stand up as a self-determined nation.

As soon as I arrived in Europe, I became a member of Amnesty International. We had meetings at our local branch once a month. One day, I went to the meeting held at the local Amnesty International Bookshop as usual, after which, another group was to meet in the same room. After my meeting, I was going through the Amnesty International bookshelves, looking for my next reading book, when a British couple in their mid-twenties, probably noticing the books that I was looking at, asked me, "Are you from the Congo?" They were waiting for their meeting to start, and I just had mine a few minutes earlier in the basement. Their group is fighting against racism and imperialism, and it turns out that the Congo was, at that moment, a central case study to demonstrate everything about imperialism and capitalism, but it didn't come up in the media. We launched into a conversation that completely changed my whole geopolitical vision.

8 to 10 million lives were lost under Leopold II, even if statistics about mass murder are often hard to prove. If even half this number of murders happened in the Congo, it would have been one of the major killing grounds before World War Two. Why are these deaths never mentioned?

In the light of my meetings and discussions with this new group, which I soon joined, I began to re-examine other events that happened through the course of my life. I realized that, like many of my compatriots, I exhibited what psychologists define as Stockholm syndrome.

Post-traumatic syndrome is not a mystery, everybody is suffering from it, and I too am suffering from it, caused by King Leopold's reign. A system of genocide was inflicted upon us with great harm and trauma, and that trauma continues in the present day. This is why it is called syndrome. I had already developed in my subconscious a system of survival, which consists of getting the sympathy of the person in power in order to keep out of danger. Going to school was all about hoping to influence the colonizer's emotions, to save my life, and the lives of those who are dear to me. In reality, it's actually just my own anxiety about standing up for my future without the colonial presence. I grew up in the environment where things were run essentially by Europeans for their benefit. Churches, schools, hospitals, businesses, companies, and even socio-cultural activities were run by white folks. In the last 4 centuries, we have been making the Europeans rich. We have produced rubber for tyres, we have produced the uranium that contributed to the Hiroshima bombing, we continue to produce among other things, the coltan for the current technology industry.

Politically a hostile environment helped to create the independence movement, which forced Belgium to change and shamed them in front of the world. In the sixties, in my opinion due to the syndrome, the independence movement wanted to take the coloniser's place and so chose to be in partnership, a part of the oppressive machine. Helping the oppressor design a better exploitation system, we started building our relationship by imitating the coloniser, and we called ourselves "evolués class". We began to tell our children to be like that. By putting people in prison, rapes and deaths, we continue the behaviour from the coloniser legacy despite conference meetings, agreements, and so on.

The invader of our land forced everyone to convert to Christianity at the end of a blade or the end of a gun barrel. They forced us to worship a false god and his false blonde-haired, blue-eyed image. No other race was robbed of their names, language, religion, culture, folklore and norms. No other race went through a holocaust longer than 500 years. No other race has had institutions created to keep them mentally enslaved and below average in society like the ones that still exist today in 2016. Every race profited and still profits from our Holocaust. Because of the stigma other people put upon us, there has been so much confusion about the culture that our political and economic behaviour, attitudes, beliefs, rituals profited them and not us. During physical incarceration and as prisoners of oppression, we were forced to pick up some psychological tools used brother to brother, brother to sister, children to parents. The severe starvation, being worked to death, beaten to death, girls not reaching puberty without being raped, boys being raped the same, and all these conditions of fear inflicted on us have affected our love, our freedom, our capacity to liberate the mind. When you brutalise someone for so long they end up identifying themselves with the brutaliser to get the pain to go away. This is what we see with some of our sisters with domestic violence. We have been so screwed up that we ask our oppressors to improve what they do. We have developed little nuances and norms to fool the master. The kind of things inflicted on us as are a result of terrorism. Our parents were moulding our behaviour by inflicting fear to keep us alive and away from the trouble.

I began to read more. The further I explored, the more it was clear the Congo was bearing a death toll of a holocaust of unprecedented dimensions. Although it was Edmund Dene Morel who had ignited a movement, he was not the first outsider to see King Leopold's Congo for what it was and to try hard to draw the world's attention to it. Up until today, no one has ever emphasised enough the amount of trauma that has been left as a legacy. King Leopold II never set foot in the Congo, just as the pilots of armed drone's aircraft never hear screams or see shattered homes or torn flesh, but the devastation of his reign have been carried right through to my generation.

I recalled one day, my sister and I went to a drama presentation, organised by schools for all students as part of our literary curriculum. I remember seeing my sister during the presentation seated with her school mates. The show went on a bit later than planned, in the end we found ourselves running behind time. One of my father's rules was that everyone within our household had to come back home by 6pm at the latest. Unfortunately, a rainstorm started just a few minutes after the end of the show and my sister made the mistake of waiting for the rain to stop before finding a way of getting back home, whereas I headed home as soon as I got out of the show through the rain. Ridiculously soaked, I got home, got changed and was getting my warm dinner when through the window, I saw my sister arrive as my father was sitting in our veranda. He enjoyed sitting there as it allowed him to have an eye on the entire compound. As my sister entered the gate and headed toward the veranda, I saw my father ordering her just with gestures to kneel down in the middle of the yard in the pouring rain. She stayed there for almost two hours as punishment for getting home late from a school activity.

My father was working for a local mining company as a builder, but before he got this job, he used to run a fish farm. He left the job and moved to town because he assaulted a bullying European man. He was one of these very proud men, not wanting to show their weaknesses, especially to the opponent. My father was also a very strict man, leading the family with strict rules about almost everything. We had to wake up at a certain time in the morning, even when we didn't have things to do. Once up, the room had to be tidied up, every child had a chore within the household and nobody was to sit in the living room when my father was in it, especially when he had visitors.

Having discussed this with my friends in the neighbourhood, and at school, my father's way of leading the family was the norm for any parent of his time who wanted his children to receive a good education, increase their chance of survival and therefore increase their chance of being the house slave who worked and often lived in the house of the slave-owner. By opening my mind, I realised that the role our history has played in producing these perceptions, images and behaviour is not addressed. We rarely look to our history to understand how we adapted our behaviour over centuries.

I believe the behaviour described above, as well as many other reactions, are in large part related to our trans-generational adaptations to survive the stifling effects associated with the past traumas of slavery raids, followed by King Leopold's private state exploitation, followed by Belgian colonisation, then the dictatorial regimes with their on-going oppressions.

Trauma is inflicted by an outside, usually violent, force, event or experience. This injury can be experienced physically, emotionally, psychologically, or spiritually. The type of events that can cause the trauma can non exhaustively be: serious road accidents, violent personal assaults, such as sexual assault, mugging or robbery, prolonged sexual abuse, violence or severe neglect, witnessing violent deaths, military combat, being held hostage and natural disasters such as severe floods or earthquakes.

When trauma is severe enough it can produce a cycle of distorted attitudes and beliefs, which also produce unwanted consequences amplified by repeated experiences of the event causing the initial trauma. This is worse when caused by human beings. The Congo experience is one of continual, violent attacks on the body, mind and spirit. Congolese men, women and children are traumatised throughout their lives and the violent attacks of the past era persist long after the so-called independence in 1960. My father was the produce of that era during which people needed to develop survival techniques to protect families and love ones. In the face of these psychological wounds, those traumatised adapted their attitude and behaviour in order to survive and these adaptations continue to manifest today. We are trying to examine these adaptations with an eye towards identifying, today, those that limit us and those that make us stronger.

Viewed through the historical lens of past experience, one may better understand my father's attack on the white man, or his desire to keep his family out of trouble by implementing strict rules which were ten times harder out in the real world. Parents had to be hyper-vigilant about the whereabouts of their children, for such hypervigilance mean survival and a better future. People learned that stroking the white man in the direction of his hair meant they were able to get on with their life peacefully.

The colonial power had to perpetuate feelings of separateness and distrust by ordering calamitous punishment of one ethnic group and setting one ethnic group against another, which is still going on today. When an ethnic group was promoted by the colonial power, people often joined in the rank of oppressor. These are just a few examples of behaviour that has roots in past traumas of all sorts and has been passed down through generations. Most of them ensured our survival at one time or another. Some of them will inhibit our ability to survive and thrive today if they are not brought to light, examined and where necessary, replaced with behaviour which promotes and maximizes our progress.

Times have changed, but we are still acting out of habit just because that is the way we grew up doing things. We haven't passed on our history; people have forgotten why we got in this situation in the first place, and what purpose it served. We have to understand the immediate history of the last three generations. We need to know why we are struggling, we need to remember our pain, we need to feel the pain and anger of our ancestors whose hands were chopped off, we need to remember the screams of the women who were raped, we need to feel all that pain as it will motivate us to make for changes and bring about a revolution. We have received our culture from our ancestors. We need to liberate those of whom we feeling the pain we need to look at them as model, not to copy the model of those who are outing us in situation.

No one should deny our ancestors' heritage. We have to keep in mind as we reclaim our Black ancestry and its rich legacy and traditions, which are phenomenal and unmatched by any of our fellow man in and around this planet, that many of our people remain in a state of mental slavery. We should study our history and create a new one for ourselves. We need to create our own social language and model to motivate our children. We need to appeal to all men and women to reclaim what we know was our central and predominant faith before the invasion, as therapeutic intervention to heal and relieve our minds, our bodies and our souls of this disease known as Post-Traumatic King Leopold Syndrome. This is a permanent war, but we don't see it as a war. We are trying to suppress "ingeta", the Congolese diaspora revolutionary movement, to please the oppressor because it is antagonising for the imperialist power.

The primary purpose of this work is to encourage Congolese and African people to view their attitudes, assumptions and behaviour through the lens of history and so gain a greater understanding of the impact that centuries of oppression and plunder has had on our lives. With this understanding, we can explore the role our history has played in the evolution of our thoughts and feelings about who and what we are as well as our beliefs about how we are to behave. While it is true that some of this evolution has resulted in behaviours that have become both destructive and ill-adapted, it is also encouraging that in spite of the plunder and oppressive conditions endured by past generations, they were able to pass on their phenomenal powers of resilience and adaptability. It is essential that we build upon these strengths in ways that will sustain and advance future generations.

Chapter 1: The Civilising Mission

"It is in vain that some philanthropists tried to prove that the Negro species is as intelligent as the white species. One indisputable fact which dominates all others, is that they have the most narrowed brain, lighter and less bulky than the white species. But this intellectual superiority that we feel cannot be doubted, does it give whites the right to enslave the inferior race? No, a thousand times no. If Negroes are closer to certain animal species by their anatomical forms, their gross instincts, they differ and are similar to white men in other respects we have to take utmost account. They are endowed with speech and word we can build with them the intellectual and moral relations, we can try to raise them up to us, and some might succeed to a certain limit. Besides, a sociological fact that we must never forget is that their race is likely to mix with ours, and striking outward sign of our common nature. Their intellectual inferiority, far from conferring us the right to abuse their weakness, imposes on us a duty to assist and protect them. « Pierre Larousse, Article «Nègre», Grand Dictionnaire Universel du 19e s. (1872).

'I have undertaken the work in Congo in the interest of civilisation and for the good of Belgium.' Monument, Arlon, Belgium.

Not long ago, a 38-year-old American who works in the mining industry and ran for Congress in 2012 began researching disputed regions across the world, because his seven-year-old daughter came to him one night and asked him if she would ever be a real princess. He figured that in order to make his daughter a princess, he would have to make himself a king. He looked at Antarctica, and there was unclaimed land there, but there was also a treaty that meant people can't claim it. So, he kept researching, and found Bir Tawil.

He flew to Africa for the express purpose of claiming the 800 square miles that make up Bir Tawil, a desert territory that falls between the borders of Egypt and Sudan. He travelled for 14 hours in a caravan in order to plant the flag designed by his children on the soil of Bir Tawil. He reckoned this act made his claim more legitimate than previous attempts he made online. He, his wife, and his three children decided to rename the territory the *Kingdom of North Sudan*, and planned to launch a website to spell out their vision for the new country. His daughter, the "Princess" has said she wants to ensure children in the region have enough food, even if Bir Tawil itself is uninhabited. Her father explained he is simply following the same process as many others have done over hundreds of years, planting out flags, and claiming lands. Does this sound familiar?

In 1876, an unremarkable monarch of an insignificant European kingdom outwitted all other powerful European countries, by claiming he would bring civilisation to the indigenous people of Africa, and made the first bold imperial move into new territory in the African interior.

King Leopold II formed the philanthropic organisation "Association Internationale Africaine" (International African Association) and became its single shareholder. Under the guise of humanitarian work and westernisation of African peoples, Leopold II used the International African Association to further his ambitions of empire building in the hope of bringing international prestige to the relatively small Belgium, when in fact he actually brought destruction, death, diseases, division, hate, cruelty and inhumanity. In reality, the International African Association was a vehicle to enslave the people of the Congo River Basin and enrich Leopold II. It was a private holding company disguised as an international scientific and philanthropic association. How could most Europeans believe that King Leopold spent his fortune funding public works in the Congo and stopping slavery there? How could they believe that his interests in Africa were altruistic and humanitarian? Because he was the unintimidating King of Belgium, cousin of Queen Victoria of England, a wealthy, noble and "philanthropic" modern king. But it was all a sham.

In the 23 years (1885-1908) that Leopold II ruled the Congo he massacred more than 10 million people by cutting off their hands and genitals, flogging them to death, starving them into forced labour, holding children ransom and burning villages. The irony is that Leopold II committed these atrocities without even setting foot in the Congo.

He convinced explorers, politicians, and newspapers alike that he intended to help Africans, though, in reality, he was driven to find some imperial territory for himself. It must be noted however, that in the same period acts of brutality were being committed on native peoples elsewhere in the world by Europeans. By Britain on the Aborigines in Australia, by the United States on native Americans and Filipinos , by the French on central and western Africans, by the Spanish on the north and central native Americans, the Portuguese on the Angolans and Amazonians, and by the Germans on southwest Africans.

Leopold hosted a Geographical Conference on Central Africa, to which he invited famous explorers to discuss ending the slave trade and spreading European civilisation. As Hochschild quoted in his book, at the conference, King Leopold appealed to the explorers' interests in an ideological quest: "To open to civilisation the only part of our globe which it has not yet penetrated, to pierce the darkness which hangs over entire peoples, is, I dare say, a crusade worthy of this century of progress".

The group founded a charitable organisation, the International African Association, with Leopold as the chairperson. The king promised to spend his own fortune to fund the enterprise. Newspapers and politicians heralded the conference throughout Europe and donations poured in. But the group never met again. Rather, Leopold used its name as a shell and cover for his private ownership of the Congo.

The strategy is still being used in present days as philanthropic funds are common among the European super rich, enabling tax avoidance provided five per cent of net investment assets are given away annually with set orientation towards the uncivilised poor. Philanthropy isn't a black-and-white issue though, and important questions have been raised about the way these foundations operate, and the impact of their work. Philanthropy seeks not just to make businesses more charitable, but to make charity more business-like, based on NGOs competing for grants with their performance evaluated using business metrics.

What man so civilised and prosperous in his own lands and amongst his own people would seek to make riches from the oppression of other men? Who would spend his hard-earned resources to subdue, murder, enslave and destroy other men with the sole mission of making them civilised? Who would actually enforce his principles of wealth on another man? King Leopold was that man, in the name of all Europeans. Differing ideas of what civilisation means have been used to justify the subjugation and enslavement of those different and less powerful since Aristotle. Such brutality and oppression in the name of civilisation has occurred so many times, over so many years, that we can no longer recognize and acknowledge the simple beauty in the diversity of the human family. The concept of civilisation has become confused with variation in skin colours and cultural expression.

With the European invasion in Africa being endorsed as legal, acceptable and justifiable, the founding fathers of the Berlin conference committed the west's original sin, a sin that has continued to plague the world to the present day. These days, the media is used to invade the mind, giving them even better results than physical occupation. A whole propaganda machine has been put in place with lot of financial resources, to carry on their subliminal messages.

The British government invests more than 600 million euros each year in the BBC (British Broadcasting Corporation), reaching about 96 million Africans every week. France spends 140 million euros a year on Radio France International known as RFI, broadcasting to 40 million Africans every week, 80 million euros per year on "France 24", which reaches 45 million African per week and finally €63 million per year on "TV5" which also reaches 55 million Africans per week. The African elite today receive information of events taking place in Africa from the European media that I just mentioned.

Africa has struggled to recover from the dehumanization of servitude, the offence of peonage, and the ravage of poverty. Only blacks are stripped of the title of being a human being all over the world. African enslavement still goes on 500 years later. They are still being forcibly taken from their land. They are still criminalized by the law and media, medically and scientifically experimented on, sometimes without anaesthesia, because they are not considered to be human and thus should not feel pain.

African families were torn apart from each other for many reasons. Africans were not allowed to congregate. They were not allowed to communicate with each other in their native tongue. Their lynching and live burnings were seen as a form of entertainment for whites who made post card photos and mailed them to distant relatives as a form of celebration. After the murder of a black person, whites often kept souvenirs such as a toe, finger, or teeth, such as the Belgian man claiming having kept Patrice Lumumba's teeth after putting his body parts in acid Modern day captivity sees thousands of blacks jailed for crimes that whites don't even get arrested for, even though blacks are statistically no more likely to be criminals than anyone else. Blacks simply face harsher punishments and penalties than anyone else.

When we look at Europe as a place, it only came into human history in the last few centuries. Not one significant contribution or level of development was accomplished before its contact with Africa; instead, the destruction of our homes, the looting of our lands and people, and the theft of our property is what European's civilisation was about. Self-knowledge is the basis or foundation of self-identity and self-respect. It is a corrective to myths and lies such as Columbus "discovered" America, or the Greeks "invented" democracy, philosophy, and science.

Africa was and still is about history, knowledge, mental capacity, understanding, resources, fertile lands, waters, climate, the sciences, the arts, and the people. African people were the first humans in the world, and began to move from Africa to Europe and Asia around 60,000 years ago. They created the first and some of the most profound civilisations in the world. No other races or ethnic groups can make these claims. They created pyramids, established the first laws and peaceful societies, organized spirituality, created mathematics and advanced medical procedures. Africans built many of the original castles in Europe, and the signs are still visible today, like the University of Salamanca. Christopher Columbus travelled to America with Africans called Moors. You will find in Africa, monuments, civilisations, cultures, artefacts, sciences and philosophies dating back tens of thousands of years. Archaeologists today note the use of Ishango Bones, currently held at the Royal Belgian Institute of Natural Sciences, Brussels, as the earliest mathematical artefact in the world; also a calculator and lunar calendar. This tool, discovered in the area of Ishango near the Semliki River at the border of Congo and Uganda in Africa, was used when conducting commercial transactions and for scientific purposes 20,000 years BC, compared to the abacus, which originated between 2400 BC and 300 BC, i.e. 17,600 - 19,700 years later. Somehow, these accomplishments are not acknowledged by western museums. No wonder, as they have tried so hard to change history and claim ancient Ethiopia (modern Egypt) was their creation.

Research demonstrates that at the height of Kongo Empire (1000 BC - 1500 AD), around central

Africa, there was an established local, regional and international trading network. Crops and fish maintained Kongo as the breadbasket of the region. Raw materials, e.g. iron and ivory were transported to the ports of Mombasa, Kilwa and Sofala from where they were shipped as far as China and India. Iron and copper technologies and ores were developed and traded. Prosperous business, financial wealth, strong government and politico-economic expansion were symbols of the Kongo Empire. The West's first introduction to Kongo's vast human and natural resources dates back to 1400, when Portuguese explorers commissioned by the Crown to look for new trade routes travelled into Central Africa.

In 1623, the Kongo Empire became the apostolic prefecture of Pope Urban VIII, until the decline of Portugal by 1644. Europeans begin utilizing Congolese trading routes for commerce in human and natural resources. Enslaved people added to the mix of goods transported along trading networks. King Nkuwu Nzinga of the Kongo Empire converted to Christianity as King João I. Mani Kongo wrote to King João III of Portugal, imploring him to cease the slave trade as it was destroying his society. So many people were sold into slavery that the empire collapsed between 1500 and 1800 due to lack of human resources and the cost of war with the Portuguese.

The devastating effect of these invasions has run like poison through the blood of the Congolese since the encounter of Europeans with the continent back as far as the 15th century. Westerners have invested much in denying the racial motive behind their enterprise. Such denial has allowed the illness to fester for centuries. At the root of this sickness is the unchallenged belief that there are physical differences between people that account for the intellectual attributes and abilities of those people.

You learn upon arrival into modern European countries that you have to apply for asylum to be able to stay. The asylum application is a long, painful and humiliating process in which it must be shown in the eyes of the immigration law, that the reason for the asylum is valid. The trajectory taken to escape has to be direct not via a third country. You must demonstrate that you are native to your country of origin, and finally demonstrate that your life is in danger if you go back.

The decision giving the right to stay can take 6 months to 10 years to be reached. Meanwhile, there is withdrawal of all benefits support from those who do not claim asylum immediately on their arrival. Even those who apply within hours are also refused support and made destitute. The destitution means the denial of the right to work and support oneself and family. To those who make it to the tight deadline, the government provides shared accommodation, with two people in the room. Asylum seekers and children are housed in poor, unfit and overcrowded housing. If you are married, you have to give evidence of your marriage, and you have no right to get married on arrival before you get the government's decision. Registrars must report 'suspect' marriages; marriage ceremonies are raided; couples are separated and non-national partner deported. Immigration snatch-squads take children from schools into detention. Babies are born in detention centres and locked up for months; their mothers are handcuffed and/or strip-searched during labour. There is a dispersal system, which sends asylum seekers to distant parts of the country, isolating them; it can also split some families up by dispersing a spouse anywhere in the country away from their partner. Asylum seekers receive no cash, only weekly paper vouchers, which also stigmatises them in local supermarkets.

There are people who after seeking asylum will be waiting for the government's decision in detention centres. These are specific prisons for immigrants. They are also called immigration removal centres but the conditions are the same as real prisons such as lack of medical care, physical abuse and isolation. Detainees are refused medical treatment or handcuffed to see doctors or dentists.

Families including pregnant mothers have their financial support and accommodation withdrawn and are made destitute; their children are taken into the care of social services in order to force and intimidate them to leave the country. Detainees who protest or are assaulted in these detention centres are quickly deported along with any potential witnesses. Immigration officers have increased powers to arrest, detain, search and seize property.

The immigration humiliation can reach its peak when people end up feeling excluded from daily social life. With lack of financial means, they cannot dream of socialising with the locals. This situation, consequently, puts people straight to the bottom of the social scale, whatever their origin or background. The social hierarchy in society is organised as a pyramid, where those nearest the top have more power and economic means than those nearest the bottom. The fact is that those at the top happen to be indigenous, and they tend to protect themselves against those at the bottom; this results in institutional racism.

People at the bottom of the social scale are living in the most deprived areas and their average wage is the national minimum wage. They are more likely to be convicted and given a custodial sentence for a first offence, more likely to be remanded in prison and to be stripped of citizenship before being removed and they are three times more likely to be stopped and search by police on a daily basis. Given all these conditions, why then do people flee their country in the first place?

Because centuries ago their invasion created this illusion of freedom and inclusiveness, described by Dr Amos as: *the freedom to speak as long as no one listens, to explain as long as no one understands, to sing and dance as long as you entertain those who would have you sing and dance on a tightrope above an open grave, to think as long as you think feelings, to love as long as it is your oppressors and not yourself that you love, to assemble as long as you gather together to screw each other, to engage in self-defence as long as it is truth and not reality against which you defend yourself.*

When material gain becomes the god before which all must be sacrificed, even one's own humanity, all manner of crimes and pursuant justifications become possible. And when crimes become heinous enough, as in wars of aggression, genocide and enslavement, the perpetrators have little choice but to dehumanise their victims. African societies were arranged based upon kinship relationships. The extended family was an interdependent unit that provided for the care of the children, the sick and the elderly. In African culture, your nieces and nephews would consider themselves brothers and sisters instead of cousins. You would never refer to your cousin as "cousin" because that would be an insult. So, your cousins are your sisters and brothers. Your nieces are your children. Your uncles are your fathers. Your aunts are your mothers. Children are encouraged to call other people outside the family mothers and fathers, sisters and brothers. The extended family structure was part of a survival strategy, particularly for Africans whose kinship ties provided the mechanism for child-rearing and social organisation. All the members of the extended family helped to provide for the basic needs of food, clothing and shelter -cooperation within a close–knit family ensured the continued existence of that particular tribe or group.

The African communities relied principally on consensus, customs and traditions rather than legislative processes. Relying on consensus confirmed that all individuals were important in determining the movement and direction of the whole group. In the African community, relationships frequently outplay everything else. Consideration of relationships permeates all interactions. For example, if a man feels they have been disrespected by their boss at work, they often feel completely justified in rebelling and shutting out the offending person, even if it means losing their job.

Throughout the sixties, 17 sub-Saharan African countries, including the Congo, gained their independence from colonial power,] as a result of a long process that began more than fifteen years earlier in the tumult of the Second World War. Ahead of the emergence of riots and to protect their own safety, the colonial administration created a segregated social class called "les évolués". An évolué, someone who literally "evolved" or "developed" during the colonial era, referred to a native Congolese who had evolved by becoming europeanised through education or assimilation and had accepted European values and patterns of behaviour.

According to that doctrine, blacks had no civilisation but a certain class of them could claim to be civilised, following a form of training that would prove awkward and humiliating for them. After training, they registered or received a civil merit card, which was the certificate of civilisation. Évolués spoke European languages, followed European laws rather than customary laws, usually held white-collar jobs, although rarely higher than clerks, and lived primarily in urban areas. These men had to break social ties with their community, and enter another system designed to exemplify the success of the civilizing mission claimed by King Leopold II. In particular, it was felt that after gaining independence in 1960, the assimilation of European values by the évolués meant that European civilian inhabitants of the Congo could continue to live in the Congo as part of a culturally European multiracial state. Just as General Janssens, commander of the Force

Publique colonial army, had said to his military: *"Before independence is equal to after independence"*, so the same struggle continued.

Many of the leaders of the nationalist parties in the Belgian Congo were members of the évolué class, looking down on their helpers or patronising them. Their position of power accessed by manumission prevented them working on common projects. When they got together, they let their egos dominate their common goals. More than fifty years after the country's newly gained independence, Patrice Emery Lumumba's speech, given as the first premier minister of Congo (and the speech for which he paid with his life), was still a vivid description of reality.

There are still tears and blood flowing across the country as a result of the humiliating slavery which was imposed on it and passed through generations. In some areas of the Congo, people are still forced to work without pay to allow them to feed and look after their families. Insults and ongoing ironies and prejudices are still alive just because of skin colour. The mining contracts continue to be illegal while plunder and looting continue. The double standards policy continues to be applied for housing, for jobs, even throughout social life such as cinemas, restaurants or shopping stores.

Today's leaders are unable to govern effectively due to the fact that the colonisers left behind hybrid people, conceived in Western laboratories, with no deep knowledge of the African culture, with no vision of the future of their people, or their country. The intellectuals and leaders continue to imitate their European masters, being used as stooges, lap-dogs and puppets to rape, loot and cause catastrophes in their own countries. They are left as consumers mostly; they act out of greed, driven by pleasure and desire for material wealth. They want to own more without saving or investing for future generations. Instead of starting enterprises, they think only of buying expensive new things. Some of them neglect their own children's education in order to obtain the latest designer clothes. People want things that give them a certain "status", once reserved for westerners only. They are happy to sit in conferences and conventions in well-known international hotels talking about what they plan to do while congratulating titled speakers and rather than the best entrepreneurs. They do not understand that there is nothing better than individual entities coming together to contribute to a common task. In reality, many of these leaders do not realise that they are only one signature away from being poor and they are two months' salary away from poverty controlled by the westerners.

There are estimates of ten million casualties as a direct consequence of King Leopold II civilising reign and it has made a profound impact upon the Congo's later development into what people refer to as a *failed state*. The Congo Free State fulfilled several of the criteria needed for development into such an atrocious regime. The combination of a comparatively small state apparatus with little resources in terms of military and economic power, controlled by a ruthless leader attempting to rule and maximise profits made from extracting the resources of a vast territory led to the use of significant administrative coercion. The colonial leadership identified the use of terror as the most cost-efficient method of imposing rule and facilitating extraction, devising a systematic approach towards the territory's population. This system of terror was structured in several layers. One of these was an incentive system indirectly rewarding the colonial administration for the use of excessive force, another was the recruitment and collaboration of different native peoples acting as soldiers for the colonial officials. As the administration's wages were directly linked to the profits made from extracted resources, it created incentives for the use of ruthless measures, linking the market mechanism with violence.

In such a country and such a climate, a bunch of rough-grained Belgian army officers, unaccustomed to the management of any other race and untrained in civil government, had absolute power over the native population, and were ordered to raise revenue to the utmost of their ability. Above them was a military autocrat as governor, sternly determined to be obeyed and to ensure his royal master's enterprise was commercially sound - and so the stage was set for exactions enforced by cruelty.

Evidence of the atrocious nature of Congo Free State is overwhelming both in the scope and the breadth of sources. Its violence derived from the policies of King Leopold II seeking profit maximisation through externalising labour costs within a legal and moral vacuum. As the rubber collection required little capital investments in the form of tools, few skills in the form of collection techniques and only modest physical fitness, it qualified a vast majority of the Congolese population to become potential labourers. Consequently, the external incentives for administrative coercion were increased through rising rubber prices, a dire financial position held by the territorial owner, the non-existence of legal protection for the natives, the incentive structure for the colonial officials, the human agency of collaborating natives and the racial ideology that served to pervert the morality of the subjugating agents. Thus a European ruler displaying no cognitive ability for empathy, gained control over a vast territory against all odds, driven by a combination of greed and financial desperation to devise a system so brutal that its reverberations are still felt today.

Chapter 2: Dehumanisation and cognitive dissonance

Human beings have a remarkable ability to dehumanize one another, to conceive of others as subhuman creatures, and to treat them accordingly. Twenty years ago, a Belgian man went to Africa. During his stay, he became interested in a black woman who was about 10 years younger than he. The woman wasn't especially beautiful so it has appeared that she had to prove her worth to the man. The man contacted the family at the end of his stay to demand her hand in marriage and take her back to Belgium. The couple lived together and had two children. That woman is now dead. One day, her children stumbled across secret documents proving that for more than twenty years, their father had carried out scientific experiments using his black wife as his guinea pig. The children decided to bring their father to justice for killing their mother.

The Great Chain of Being is a concept that dates back to Plato and Aristotle. It is a strict, religious hierarchical structure of all life, and it is believed to have been decreed by God. The chain starts with God at the top as the perfect being with inert matter at the bottom, and every living creature situated at some intermediate position. Europeans had placed themselves near the uppermost rank, and had supposed that every other creature was less than human. This is how European colonialists conceived of Blacks Africans, and how slave owners conceived of their human chattel.

When we bring up the issues of King Leopold's slavery system, all too often we are met with these words: "C'mon now, this happened ages ago, today you are your own masters why can't you turn things around?" or, "!Why do you talk about colonisation? That was back then." Or you'll hear Europeans offering, "Well, we don't have anything to do with that anymore." They do not recognise that they are still living off the interest of the wealth that their forefathers earned from that system. They are still enjoying the accumulated wealth that began with that enslavement.

At The Berlin Conference of 1884–85, also known as the Congo Conference, Europeans regulated the colonization in Africa. Its outcome, the General Act of the Berlin Conference, can be seen as the formalization of the Scramble for Africa, which eliminated or overrode most existing forms of African autonomy and self-governance. They viewed black people as a lesser species of human than those of European descent. This way of thinking was reflected in dehumanizing epithets. In dehumanizing others, they were excluded from the circle of moral obligation. They could then be killed, oppressed, and enslaved with impunity. Taking the life of a dehumanized person became of no greater consequence than crushing an insect under one's boot.

Why did the humanity of black people come into question? Possibly because when we commit a negative act or think about doing so, most of us become uncomfortable. This discomfort is caused by the difference between our actions and what we believe about ourselves. Also, most of us think of ourselves as decent people and decent people do not do evil things. This discomfort is called "cognitive dissonance". The bigger the difference between our actions and what we think about ourselves, the greater the cognitive dissonance and so, our discomfort. People do not particularly like this discomfort; they often try to resolve it immediately whenever it occurs.

The other way to deal with it is to justify the negative act rather than admit any wrongdoing. In instances of particularly egregious negative acts like wars of aggression, enslavements and genocides the perpetrators have to go so far as to demonise and in many cases, dehumanise their victims. Dehumanisation describes the denial of "humanness" to other people. It is theorized to take on two forms: animalistic dehumanisation, which is employed on a largely intergroup basis, and mechanistic dehumanization, which is employed on a largely interpersonal basis. It can occur discursively such as in idiomatic language that likens certain human beings to animals, verbal abuse and erasing one's voice from discourse, symbolically as imagery, or else physically as chattel slavery, physical abuse, etc.

Children accompanying their parents on a protest shouted "Monkey, eat your banana!" at the French former minister Taubira, and a priest on a Catholic fundamentalist demonstration linked her to an old advertisement for the chocolate drink "Banania", which many consider racist. Dehumanisation may be carried out by a social institution such as a state, school, or family, interpersonally, or even within the self. State-organized dehumanization has been directed against black populations around the globe and was facilitated by status, power, and social connection.

By the early 1880s, European interest in the continent had increased dramatically on recognition of Africa's abundance of valuable resources such as gold, timber, land, markets and labour power. There was no disputing the fact that dehumanisation and atrocity often went hand in hand. It has been used to explain and justify the aggressive actions of Europeans that systematically turned the capturing, shipping and selling of other human beings into a business, a business that would develop into backbone of an entire economy, providing the foundation for the world's wealthiest nations.

During the past 600 years, white supremacists have spent significant resources to prove black people and those of African descent are inferior. Unkind opinions, beliefs, half-truth and outright lies have been presented over the years to prove blacks are inferior to whites. Many of these were printed in textbooks, scientific journals and media. The effort to prove white superiority goes on to this very day and it is important for us to be able to differentiate fact from fiction. These efforts have been so successful that many white people believe it and act accordingly. Even more telling, many black people appear to believe it as well. The "scientific" theories on the classification of populations and racial inequality considered the native Africans as backward or primitive populations in order to justify the "civilizing" mission.

From the 1870s, a new wave of colonization developed in Africa. Proponents of an imperialist policy that is to say, conquest and expansion of new land as far as it is based;

"Open to civilisation the only part of the world where it has not yet penetrated, pierce the darkness that envelop the entire populations is if I dare say, a crusade worthy of this century of progress. It's comes to plant the standard of civilisation on the soil of Central Africa and to fight against the slave trade.

In King Leopold II's opening speech of the Brussels Conference of Geography in 1876 he said to colonise is to liaise with new countries and to enjoy the resources of any kind in those countries. , At the same time, it was in the national interest to bring to those primitive peoples the benefits of intellectual culture and the social, scientific, moral, artistic, literary, commercial and industrial prerogatives of superior races. Colonisation is therefore an institution founded in nine countries by an advanced race, to achieve the double purpose that we have indicated. Some philanthropists have tried in vain to prove that the negro species is as intelligent as the white kind. A few examples will illustrate this point.

'An indisputable fact that dominates all others, is that they have a brain that is narrower, lighter and less bulky than the white species, and as in the whole animal series, intelligence is in direct proportion brain sizes, the number and depth of the convolutions, which is sufficient to prove the superiority of the white species over the black.' This was an article published in Larousse, 1863-1865, the Great

Universal Dictionary of the nineteenth century.

'There is more difference from man to man than animal to man. (...) Go see these monstrous sons of Equatorial Africa; you will surely have the impression that the abyss is less among the dogs that bark nearby and an Ashanti,' said Jules Lemaitre, a French writer and ultranationalist in 1887.

'The white man must fulfil a mission, spreading civilisation from Europe among the lower races, among savages. Nature has made a race of workers, the Chinese race, who have wonderful manual dexterity and almost no sense of honour... A race of tillers of the soil, the Negro; treat him with kindness and humanity, and all will be as it should; a race of masters and soldiers, the European race. Reduce this noble race to working in the <u>ergastulum</u> *like Negroes and Chinese, and they rebel... But the life at which our workers rebel would make a Chinese or a negro* <u>fellah</u> *happy, as they are not military creatures in the least. Let each one do what he is made for, and all will be well.'* - Ernest Renan, the intellectual and moral reformist, in 1871.

'I repeat that the superior races have a right because they have a duty. They have the duty to civilize the inferior races. It is therefore necessary to illuminate these populations. This education involves learning the language, but also of history, but not just any, that of the metropolis,' -Jules Ferry in his famous speech to MPs July 28, 1885.

The idea that "the African" indulged in idleness and was naturally lazy took shape when the Europeans wanted to use its workforce as part of the slave trade. The stereotype developed during the colonial period. From the beginning of the conquest, the colonising states needed labour for pottering, for the execution of work equipment. The harsh working conditions and poor remuneration did not attract local farmers. Also, the colonial governments used various ways to get the workers they needed. The system benefits or chores were accompanied by numerous abuses. With labour remaining insufficient, the administration resorted to forced labour, which was not met with enthusiasm by the native populations. However, many settlers justified the use of forced labour by the need to civilize Africans. At the time, elementary education was sometimes provided in native languages, but secondary and higher education was always in the language of the coloniser.

The following excerpt from a textbook used by Brothers of St. Gabriel, a convent in the Belgian Congo back in 1937 explains everything. It is important to know that this book was written in Lingala, the most used vernacular in Congo and this is a lesson entitled "Congolese". It said, *Congo is a big country containing forests and waters. God has provided a lot of animals to feed people. Black people live in Congo. Formerly they were wild, but now their intelligence has developed rapidly. We notice a lot of money is going through the hands of workers. Some blacks are able to buy bicycles or sewing machines. But the wealth of the land is worthless before God. The priests arrived in black to teach faith in God. Many blacks converted to their teaching. That's why we meet many good Christians in Congo. Priests heal the souls of blacks, doctors treat the body of patients. In truth, the land of Congo is progressing on the path of education. We thank God for sending the Belgians to our country."*

The difference between the actions of the Europeans such as enslaving, raping, sexual abuses and killing and their beliefs about themselves as good Christians was so great and the cognitive dissonance so painful, that they were obliged to go to great lengths in order to survive their own horrific behaviour.

Scientific determinism of classical physics was used as a crutch to rationalise the prejudices of the age, to the point of creating human zoos; an era of racial superiority and the invention of the savage. Putting the 'primitive' on display began when explorers like Columbus and Vespucci lured natives back to Europe from their homelands. To prove the discovery of exotic lands, the natives were flaunted and paraded like trophies.

A 20-year-old girl from South Africa known as Sarah Baartman would be emblematic of the dark era that gave rise to the popularity of human zoos. With her protuberant buttocks and elongated labia, she was recruited in Cape Town and travelled to

London in 1810 to take part in an exhibition. The young woman went willingly under the pretence that she would find wealth and fame. She found herself being exhibited in cages at sideshow attractions dressed in tight-fitting clothing that violated any cultural norms of decency at the time. A few years later, she came to Paris where racial anthropologists poked and prodded and made their theories. She had been in Europe for only four years; to support herself Sarah eventually turned to prostitution and drank heavily. When she died in poverty, Sarah's skeleton, sexual organs and brain were put on display at the Museum of Mankind in Paris where they remained until 1974. President Nelson Mandela formally requested the repatriation of her remains, nearly two hundred years later, in 2002.

The Belgian Government intended to show the benefits of the colonial project led by King Leopold II to the public. The support of the public was as essential as that of investors. A team of Belgian doctors therefore went to Congo. They pulled out from the "jungle" no less than 267 individuals from varied ethnic groups. After a month-long journey, which cost the lives of four passengers, they finally arrived at the Antwerp Port in June 1897. Ceremonies, parades, marching bands and fireworks were held to show off the African guests dressed for the occasion. They were housed in boxes in the

Tervuren buildings where they received food, beer and even gin to warm them up.

During the day, the Congolese had to re-enact their African lives in front of boxes made with materials brought from there and planted in the park, along the ponds. Fences separated the visitors, which numbered one million. However, bad weather was already topical at the time, and black people would be victims of epidemics unfamiliar diseases such as influenza and pneumonia, and seven of them died: Mama Sambo, Mama Mpemba, Mama Ngemba, Tata Ekia, Tata Nzau, Tata Kitukwa and Tata Mibange. Note that they were not allowed to carry the normal titles of Sir, Mister or Mrs, hence the titles such as Mama or Tata.

Even once they were dead, dishonour pursued them because there was no place to bury them, no place for them in Belgian graves. At the same time, there was huge fear of coming into contact with these bodies and so they were initially buried in a common grave, which they had to share with destitute of the time. This was done in the wood of Tervuren. There was still no room for them in Belgian cemeteries. The slavery experience was exclusively based on the notion of racial inferiority. Black people were considered presumed or natural slaves based on their skin colour. They were also referred to as thinking property and inherently rightless persons.

Europeans concluded that by a natural act of God blacks belonged in the position of permanent oppression. It was this regulation to lesser humanity that allowed the institution of chattel slavery to be intrinsically linked with violence, and it was through violence, aggression and dehumanisation that the institution of colonialism was enacted, legislated and perpetuated by Europeans.

The ideology of racism opened the door to mass murders, torture, rape, disease and enslavement. What made racism even more odious was that it was rooted firmly in the soil of capitalism. Racism was and is, simply a means to an end. This is how anyone can kill ten million black people, as King Leopold did, and get away with it. Most people haven't heard of him. But they should have. He "bought" the Congo and enslaved its people, turning the entire country into his own personal slave plantation. He disguised his business transactions as "philanthropic" and "scientific" efforts under the banner of the International African Society. He used their enslaved labour to extract Congolese resources and services. His reign was enforced through work camps, body mutilations, executions and torture by his private army.

Most of us, aren't taught about him in school. We don't hear about him in the media. He's not part of the widely repeated narrative of oppression, which includes things like the Holocaust during World War II. When we learn about Africa, we learn about a caricaturized Egypt, about the HIV epidemic (but never its causes), yet we don't learn about the Great African War or Leopold's Reign of Terror and the Congolese genocide.

Stories which support the white supremacists' narrative regarding the sub-humanness of African people are allowed to be entered into the records of history. However, the European who turned the Congo into his own personal part-plantation, part-concentration camp, part-Christian ministry and killed 10 to 15 million Congolese people in the process doesn't feature. Leopold was just one part of thousands of things that helped construct white supremacy as both an ideological narrative and material reality. Of course, he was not the source of all evil in the Congo. He had generals, foot soldiers and managers who did his bidding and enforced his laws. It was a system. However, that doesn't negate the need to talk about the individuals who are symbolic of the system. Yet since the effects of capitalism in Africa are not discussed, all the privileges that rich colonialists gained from the Congolese genocide are hidden. The victims of imperialism are made, as is often the case, invisible.

One of the most puzzling phenomena in Africa is that of endemic violence, which cuts across pre-colonial, colonial and postcolonial epochs. It is easy to understand manifestations of violence within situations such as pre-colonial raiding, colonial wars of conquest and nationalist resistance wars, but there are many other forms whose logic is harder to understand such as terrorism, xenophobia, racist-inspired violence, criminality, rape, torture and maiming.

Firstly, race was used not only to subordinate black people, but also to deny their very humanity, to justify any forms of oppressive violence such as slavery, colonial conquest, dispossession, imprisonment, rape, and killing. People were defined as inferior and hence obstacles to their own economic, religious and social civilisation, in many cases justifying the suspension of normal ethical conventions. The lighter one's skin is, the closer to full humanity one is, and vice versa. As the conquerors took on the role of mapping the world, they kept reproducing this vision of things. The whole world was seen in the light of this logic. African nationalism then reproduced that oppressive violence and authoritarianism, in the name of national unity, security and postcolonial development, which was seen as necessary to secure a postcolonial modernity, as a mode of governance.

The racist, imperial scepticism that existed questioned the very humanity of Congolese people, which was a deliberate strategy to justify interventions on their land, enslaving and domesticating them like animals and treating them as usable and dispensable beings. As they were considered to have no souls, it meant that the ethics, laws and other social sanctions that regulated life in Europe and other Western parts of the world could be suspended and the law of nature including oppressive violence became legitimate.

At another level, the introduction of Western religion in Africa was also based on an imperial attitude that viewed black people as without religion. Such people were not considered to be complete human beings. Ideas of race, religion and empire reinforced each other. When adventurers like Henry Morton Stanley emphasized that the people they encountered had no religion, they were justifying a particular form of oppression rooted in the notion of black people as empty beings lacking sensibility and ready for indoctrination with Christianity. To acquire Congo, King Leopold II hired Henry Morton Stanley, who cheated African chiefs into signing away their land and power under the guise of treaties of friendship.

King Leopold II of Belgium turned Congo into his personal *'massive labour camp'*, where *'in the distinction between the law of persons and the law of things, the Congolese people were nothing but providers of cheap labour'*. His ventures into the Congo were from start to finish a catalogue of chicanery, violence and genocide.

Chapter 3: Crimes against humanity

Crimes against humanity are defined as acts that are committed as part of a widespread or systematic attack directed against any civilian population. Unlike war crimes, crimes against humanity can be committed during peace or war. They are not isolated or sporadic events, but are part either of a government policy or of a wider practice of atrocities tolerated or condoned by a government or a de facto authority.

In Congo, land is fundamental to indigenous people, both individually and collectively. Each individual belonged to certain territories within the family group and had spiritual connections and obligations to particular motherland. Consequently. land was not owned but one belonged to the land. Indigenous people experienced the land as a richly symbolic and spiritual landscape rather than merely a physical environment. Complex and sophisticated kinship systems placed each person in relationship to every other person in the groups and determined the behaviour of an individual to each person. Concepts of indigenous land ownership were and are different from European legal systems. While the Great Powers competed for territory elsewhere, the king of one of Europe's smallest countries carved his own private colony out of 100km2 of land. It was a vast territory which "if superimposed on the map of Europe", says Hochschild, "would stretch from Zurich to Moscow to central Turkey. It was bigger than England, France, Germany, Spain and Italy combined. Although mostly rainforest and savannah, it also embraced volcanic hills and mountains covered by snow and glaciers, some of whose peaks reached higher than the Alps."

King Leopold II, who ran the Congo Free State as his personal fiefdom from 1885 to 1908 sent instructions to Stanley to purchase as much land as he was be able to obtain, to place all the chiefs from the mouth of the Congo to the Stanley Falls under Leopold's name as soon as possible. Land rights treaties were to be as brief as possible and in a couple of articles must grant the King everything. Stanley secured 450 such agreements.

Murder; massacres; dehumanization; extermination; human experimentation; extrajudicial punishments; death squads; military use of children; kidnappings; unjust imprisonment; slavery; torture; rape; political, racial or religious persecution and other inhumane acts reached the threshold of crimes against humanity under the rule of the Belgian King

Leopold II in the 19th and early 20th centuries. It was a widespread and systematic practice, which left up to 10 million Congolese killed in one of the greatest acts of mass murder in human history. This happened because black people were stripped of the title of being human throughout the entire world. Their lives simply did not matter enough: a death toll of up to 10 million would surely not have been tolerated elsewhere. For the westerners, it was a country of little strategic importance where millions died.

Physical violence was widespread. This violence, and the accompanying murders and massacres, pushed indigenous people away from their traditional lands, where their spiritual heart belonged. It prevented them from conducting the essential ceremonies that ensured the continuing life cycles. The abduction of indigenous women and children for both economic misuse and sexual abuse was common. Racism was endemic. Death from sexual abuse of women and children was the least discussed, most hidden, and most sinister cause of death and depopulation. At times deaths of indigenous females from venereal diseases and sexually related violence outnumbered all other causes of death.

Along the banks of the Congo rivers, the villagers were requisitioned for paddling and cutting wood. They were also to provide any administrative or military officer, at their request, food and poultry. Plantations made by the inhabitants themselves were requisitioned. The porters were not fed and roamed 80-100 km torn by hunger; they arrived exhausted and sick. To escape being recruited as porters, people ran away. These desertions were punished by up to 50 "chicotte" shots, imprisonment, fines, deportation and death. To obtain the necessary porters at any cost, women and children were taken hostage, locked in boxes and intentionally not fed until the men came forward. An unknown percentage of them died of hunger there, in the place of detention. The people fled, many villages were plundered or burnt; regions bordering the rivers were devastated. During expeditions, soldiers were instructed to bring back a hand or head for each bullet fired, to make sure that none had been wasted or hidden for use in rebellions. A soldier with the chilling title "keeper of hands" accompanied each expedition.

Delivery of a certain amount of rubber was compulsory and a specified amount of points was allocated for a given number of inhabitants, which benefitted the concessionary companies even more than the colonial administration. Men and women were forced to become go and collect rubber and on their return to the village, they had to filter and wash it. When the first orders for rubber were instigated, the inhabitants had at first refused to participate, fleeing or hiding in the surrounding bushes and caves where they dodged the grenade blows. The method used by the soldiers was to arrive at a village in canoes, the inhabitants of which invariably bolted upon their arrival. The soldiers were then landed, and commenced looting, taking all the chickens, grain etc., out of the houses, after which they attacked the natives until able to seize their women. These women were kept as hostages until the chief of the district brought in the required number of kilograms of rubber. At this point, the women were sold back to their owners for a couple of goats apiece, and this continued from village to village until the requisite amount of rubber had been collected.

If the men of the village resisted the demands for rubber it meant the death of their wife, child or chief. In the rubber regions, people had to gain a state permit to travel outside their villages. Labourers wore a numbered metal disk, so a record could be kept of their individual quota. Hundreds of thousands of desperate and exhausted men carried huge baskets on their heads for up to twenty miles a day. One of the officers wrote in his diary: *"I made war against them. One example was enough: a hundred heads cut off, and there have been plenty of supplies ever since. My goal is ultimately humanitarian. I killed a hundred people... but that allowed five hundred others to live."*

Soldiers were slaves who had been press-ganged

through hostage taking, or stolen as children and brought up in child colonies founded by the King and the Catholic Church. Religion was based on a philosophy of oneness with the natural environment. Both men and women were involved in the spiritual life of the group. While men were always acknowledged as having the predominant responsibilities for the spiritual activities of the groups, past scholars studying cultures have neglected women's roles. Women's roles in traditional contexts, how these were disrupted during colonisation, and the misrepresentation of these roles, have become important issues. This practice became important during colonisation, when indigenous people attempted to bring outsiders into their kinship systems, particularly through relationships with women. Kinship systems determined exactly how one should behave towards every other person according to their relationship, so there were codes of behaviour between each person outlining their responsibilities and obligations towards others. For instance, a man had responsibilities to his nephews; he taught them hunting skills and led them through initiation. Kinship relations determined how food and gifts should be divided, who were one's teachers, who one could marry. In a sense, an individual was not alone; kinship systems placed each person securely in the group. People had defined roles according to age and gender. For example, a man's role involved skills in hunting as well as cultural obligations that were important to the cohesion of the group. Likewise a woman also had an important role; she provided most of the food for the group, was responsible for early child rearing, and also had cultural obligations. Reciprocity and sharing were and still are important characteristics in African society.

But administrators were appointed to become the legal guardian of all indigenous people, wiping out all cultural customs. They could authorise marriage and adoption at the flick of a pen. They could decide that a husband would be sent to one place, his wife to another, and his children to a dormitory at another location.

To destroy indigenous culture had political and economic roots as well as cultural and religious motives: demoralizing the enemy was also destabilizing, and weaker enemies, i.e. colonial subjects were easier to defeat and control. This legislation enforced dependency whilst denying essential services. It gave power to people who used it abusively. It tore families apart. It destroyed any sense of self-worth and value in culture, as it outlawed ceremonial processes and the use of language.

Missionaries declared indigenous people as heathens and 'tried to save their souls'. These missionaries attempted to systematically eradicate what they viewed as heathen practices and beliefs. Traumatised indigenous people were powerless to stop this form of structural and institutional violence. Psychosocial domination, or cultural genocide, occurs when oppressors believe that the oppressed are non-persons, with no culture of identity as human beings, or with a culture and identity that is inferior. They deny the oppressed the right to a separate identity as a group, or as individuals within the group. The oppressed came to believe this about themselves.

The removal of indigenous children from their families and their placement on missions, or with Europeans families, not only caused immense distress, but also facilitated the destruction of cultural beliefs and practices. Cultural genocide not only works to destroy the cultures of oppressed peoples, it also eradicates the sense of worth, of self-worth, and of well-being in individuals and groups so that they are unable to function from either their own cultural relatedness, or from the culture of the oppressors. They worked day and night on the indigenous population developing the old trick of divide and rule with tribes and manumission. People were prevented from planning their lives beyond a year. They found ways to mount tribes against each other and encourage murders among them.

European settlers were recruited from prison's

death rows or the army and brought diseases that wiped out large numbers of indigenous people, as they had no immunity to European diseases. The survivors soon existed at starvation levels, since they were unable to collect food because of illness or because they were denied access to their traditional hunting grounds by the invaders.

Leopold attempted to destroy the evidence: for eight days in 1908 furnaces in Leopold's Brussels headquarters were at full blast, as Congo State archives were turned to ash. He sent word to his agent in the Congo to do likewise. This, the "politics of forgetting", was followed by the entire Belgian state. Leopold, in the meantime, tried to ensure that his crimes would never make it into the history books. Shortly after the turnover of the colony, Hochschild writes that the furnaces near Leopold's palace burned for eight days, "turning most of the Congo state records to ash and smoke." "I will give them my Congo," the king is reported saying, "but they have no right to know what I did there."

The wrongs done to the Congo people originate from the substitution of commerce, a system based upon the right of a European State to expropriate the Native from his land and from the produce of the land, which the native alone can gather, and which modern industrialism requires. A country which is awash with precious minerals should be a source of huge domestic wealth, but is instead a magnet for armed profiteers.

All throughout slavery, then colonisation, black people were subjected to cruel and inhuman medical studies and experiments. There were surgeries on women without using any anaesthesia. To concoct a sterilization agent that would work only in blacks and that could be hidden, patients were given overdoses of anaesthetic under the guise of testing. High doses of chemotherapy were used on black breast-cancer patients, without their knowledge or consent, whilst infant patients were injected with lethal doses of morphine. In short, a number of high-profile Western medical miscreants had intentionally administered deadly agents to lots of patients under the guise of providing health care or conducting research.

Such events have spread a fear of medicine throughout Africa, even in countries where Western doctors have not practiced in significant numbers. The distrust of Western medicine has had direct consequences with many people avoiding vaccinations, believing that the vaccines are contaminated with the human immunodeficiency virus (HIV) or are actually sterilization agents in disguise. These accusations are far from paranoid. They led to the South African President Thabo Mbeki being ousted from his position because he refused to sign the antiretroviral (ARV) drugs deal.

He wanted clarity on how HIV virus is developed. He asked scientists to prepare a report on how the virus started and how antiretroviral (ARV) drugs would work. He also addressed the issue of poverty as a main core of the deaths of H.I.V. people. He said there was no point giving people pills while they have nothing to eat. Thabo Mbeki researched about how America planned to depopulate the planet of black people, the target being Africa and Brazil. After that report, Mbeki presented the case to the court but they said those books were unofficial books so his argument was not valid. After that, they were unsettled about him being exposed to such information. Manto Shabalala Msimang, Thabo Mbeki's minister of health advised people to eat healthily and use natural herbs instead of antiretroviral (ARV) drugs. Her view on treating South Africa's AIDS epidemic was to use easily accessible beverages and vegetables such as garlic and beetroot, rather than antiretroviral drugs. She became the subject of international criticism for upsetting pharmaceutical multinationals companies. The media ridiculed her, labelling her Mrs. Beetroot. She later had a controversial death; the report of the cause of her death was classified. Western Pharmaceutical companies were not prepared to lose billions through antiretroviral (ARV) drugs that patients will have to use for at least 15 years.

Huge damage was done to the psyche of the African race by White supremacist enslavers using religion, such as Christianity and Islam. That is where the racially doctored Exodus story about the curse by the Hebrew God, Yahweh, came from. The first Bible published by Johannes Gutenberg coincided with the advent of the slave trade, and all sorts of notions were incorporated in the Bible to promote White hegemony and defend the enslavement of black people. Those putting the Bible together twisted the ancient non-racial African Exodus myth by trying to say Africans are inferior; they are not human beings and, therefore, have no rights. They are cursed beings for others to trample upon, enslave, and use as beasts of burden, without compensation of any sort.

King Leopold's speech in 1885 to the evangelist colonisers being groomed for their African tasks, perfectly summarised how he and his race used their religion, Christianity, to brainwash and destroy the African:

"The Reverend father and dear compatriots: the task that is given to you to fulfil is very delicate and requires much tact. You will certainly evangelise; but your evangelisation must inspire above all, Belgium interests. Your principal objective in our mission in the Congo is never to teach the niggers to know about God. This they know already. They speak and submit to a Mungu, one Nzambi, one Nzakomba (African

gods) and what else I don't know. They know that to kill, to sleep with someone else's wife, to lie and to insult is bad. Have courage to admit it; you are not going to teach them what they know already. Your essential role is to facilitate the task of administrators and industrialists, which means you will go to interpret the gospel in the way it will best protect your interest in that part of the world. For these things, you have to keep watch on dis-interesting our savages from the richness that is plenty in their underground, to avoid that they get interested in it, and make you murderous competition and dream one day to overthrow you. Your knowledge of the gospel will allow you to find texts ordering and encouraging your followers to love poverty. Like, happier are the poor because they will inherit heaven and it's very difficult for the rich to enter the kingdom of God. You have to detach from them and make them disrespect everything, which gives courage to affront us. I make reference to their mystic system and that fetish warfare protection, which they pretend not to want to abandon, and you must do everything in your power to make it disappear. Your action will be directed essentially at the younger ones, for they won't revolt when the recommendation of the priest is contradictory to their parent's teachings. The children have to learn to obey what the missionary recommends, who is the father of their souls. You must singularly insist on their total submission and obedience. Avoid developing the spirits in the schools, teach students to read and not to reason. Recite everyday happy are those who are weeping because the kingdom of God is for them. Convert always the Blacks by using the whip.

Keep their women in nine months of submission to work freely for us. Force them to pay you in a sign of recognition, goats, chickens or eggs, every time you visit their villages, and make sure that the niggers never become rich. Sing every day that it is impossible for the rich to enter heaven. Make them pay tax each week at Sunday mass. Use the money supposed for the poor to build our own flourishing business centres. Institute a confessional system, which allows you to be good detectives, denouncing any Black that has a different consciousness contrary to that of the decision makers. Teach the niggers to forget their heroes and to adore only ours. Never present a chair to a Black that comes to visit you. Don't give him more than one cigarette. Never invite him for dinner even if he gives you a chicken every time you arrive at his house. There, dear compatriots are some of the principles you must apply. You will find many other books, which will be given to you at the end of this conference. Evangelize the niggers so that they stay forever in submission to the White colonialist, so that they will never revolt against the restraints they are undergoing."

King Leopold II of Belgium's speech perfectly sums up the essence of slavery and colonialism and our relationship with the White race ever since. Any African who reads the above statement by King Leopold II, and does not feel a sickening revulsion for Christianity and Islam, is either an illiterate pretending to be able to read, or needs the help of a psychiatrist, because he hates himself.

The Belgians and Americans, working at

maximum speed in less than ten years, mined (stole) all the uranium of the then Belgian Congo and stockpiled it at Oolen in Belgium. In the same spirit, the Shinkolobwe mines in Zaire were emptied, having supplied the major part of the uranium that went into the Nagasaki and Hiroshima bombing.

Some people were beaten or whipped to death for failing to meet the rigid production quotas for ivory and rubber harvests, imposed by Leopold's agents. Some were worked to death, forced to labour in slavelike conditions as porters, rubber gatherers or miners for little or no pay. Some died of the diseases introduced and spread throughout the Congo by Europeans. Others still died from the increasingly frequent famines that swept the Congo basin as Leopold's army rampaged through the countryside, appropriating food and crops for its own use while destroying villages and fields.

Chapter 4: Congo's Post King Leopold II Traumatic Syndrome

"The truth is that when you are at the bottom of a deep, dark pit, there is nowhere to look but up. Contemplating how you might climb out and what you will do when you get there." Brian Klems in The Writer's Dig.

The Congolese national trauma is a crisis combined with tragic experiences, which have affected the spirit of the whole nation over generations. There have been large-scale wars, genocide, and transport disasters, the assassination of leaders, and conflict situations with catastrophic effects on the health and well-being of the nation. Communities and families have been destroyed with oppression, and it has disrupted the development of the social and economic fabric of the entire nation, with effects of long-term physical and psychological harm to children and adults, as well as a reduction in material and human capital. The death toll estimated at 10 million people during Leopold II era, has been the "tip of the iceberg". Other consequences, besides death, are not well documented. They include endemic poverty, malnutrition, disability, socio-economic decline and psychosocial illness, to mention only a few. Women have an increased vulnerability to the psychological consequences of oppression, despite which their resilience under stress and their role in sustaining the families has been recognized.

What we see in today's Congo could be the result of generation upon generation of young men not being allowed the power and authority to parent their own children. Adapting to a lifetime of torture may create mothers who teach their children to adapt in the same way. Children receive most of their attitudes, life skills and approaches to life from their parents. Bear in mind that the indigenous family existed only to serve the master and in order to survive physically, psychologically and socially; the family had to develop a system which made survival possible under degrading conditions. Society prepared the young to accept exploitation and abuse, to ignore the absence of dignity and respect for themselves as human. The social, emotional and psychological price of this adjustment is what is well known today in Congo.

Times have changed, but people are still behaving out of habit. They haven't passed on their history; people have forgotten why they got in this situation in the first place, and what purpose it served. In addition to the family, the legacy of trauma is also passed down through the community.

During King Leopold's era, the Congolese community was a suppressed and marginalised group. Today, the nation is made up of individuals and families who collectively share anxiety and adaptive survival behaviours passed down from prior generations, many of whom likely suffered from Post-traumatic Stress Disorder.

Congolese people have inherited the behaviour, attitudes, beliefs and rituals set to benefit the enslavers, as containment methods, turning them into ignorant, materialistic and self-interested.

Despite the fact that we now live in the information age, where there is the opportunity to read any book, any articles, on any subject through the efforts of the fight for freedom, many Congolese refuse to read. If the information doesn't come across the television, radio or internet musical shows, then most people don't know what is going on.

After colonial independence in 1960, the country had a strong economic system with a strong currency at their disposal; they spent it all in lavish superficial luxury. Anyone with light skin can use the country today as their target market and any business venture they care to dream up, no matter how eccentric, the Congolese will buy into it. The Congolese have become primarily a country of consumers, functioning totally by insatiability. They continually want more, with little thought for saving or investing. They would rather buy new designer clothes than invest in starting a business. I know people from my community who are even neglecting their families to have the latest designer clothes, and who still think that having a flash car and a big house gives them a higher status, or that they have achieved their dream.

The Congolese rulers, mainly descendants of the former "classe des privilegiés", have created a class that looks down on their people or aids them in a condescending manner. Their self-interest does not allow them to be able to work together on any project or endeavour of substance. When they do get together, their self-interest lets their egos get in the way of their goal. Their so-called political party seems only to want to promote their name without making any real change in their community. They are content to sit in conferences and conventions in luxurious hotels, and talk about what they will do, while they award plaques to the best speakers, not to the best achievers. They do not understand that they are no better than each other because of what they own and that in reality they are always just two months away from poverty. This then is how the legacy of trauma has been transmitted.

Given the history, should we be surprised that issues of abuse, ineffectual parenting, violence and educational disillusionment continue to plague

Congolese communities today? Should we be surprised if western multinationals continue to reap profits without using physical oppression upon the Congolese community? Many of these dysfunctional adaptations can be linked to the crimes visited upon our ancestors. These are some of the manifestations of Post-Traumatic Slave-Colonial Syndrome, which I call in this writing the post –traumatic King Leopold II syndrome.

The post-traumatic King Leopold II syndrome theory suggests that centuries of slavery followed by systemic racism and oppression have resulted in multi-generational adaptive behaviours - some of which have been positive and reflect resilience and others are harmful and destructive. The theory focuses on the suffering and trauma associated with the invasion of the Congo from 1480, including periods of capture, transport, exploration, slavery, colonization, and independence up to the present time. It explains the etiology of many adaptive survival behaviours in Congolese communities across the country and the diaspora. It is a condition that exists because of the multigenerational oppression suffered by the Congolese indigenous and their descendants resulting from the centuries of slavery based on the belief in genetic inferiority and the inequalities that prevail to this day. Congo is still suffering from Post-traumatic syndrome.

Caused by King Leopold II's invasion, trauma has led to fragmented and fractured identities that in turn contribute to the escalation of violence between people. The future feels meaningless, and people articulate their felt sense of powerlessness and lack of life purpose in violent acts on themselves and others, relationships are destroyed and communities fragmented. When you experience a traumatic event, your body's defences take effect and create a stress response, which may make you feel a variety of physical symptoms, behave differently and experience more intense emotions. Directly after the event people may also experience shock and denial. This can give way over several hours or days to a range of other feelings such as sadness, anger and guilt.

One of the most insidious and pervasive symptoms of trauma spotted in Congolese community, is the adoption of the slave master's value system. At this system's foundation is the belief that Europeans, and all things associated with Caucasians, are superior; and that black, and all things associated with blackness, are inferior.

We can easily relate the above situation to a condition known as Stockholm syndrome, or capture-bonding, the psychological phenomenon in which hostages express empathy and sympathy and have positive feelings toward their captors, sometimes to the point of defending and identifying with the captors. These feelings are generally considered irrational in light of the danger or risk endured by the victims, who essentially mistake any lack of abuse from their captors for an act of kindness. However, if these feelings persist, they can lead to more serious mental health problems such as post-traumatic stress disorder (PTSD). Mental health includes our emotional, psychological and social wellbeing, and affects how we think, feel and act. It also helps determine how we handle pressure, relate to others, and make choices. It doesn't always stay the same. It can change as circumstances change and as people move through different stages of the life. People experiencing PTSD can feel anxious for years after the trauma, whether or not they were physically injured.

Stockholm syndrome can be seen as a form of traumatic bonding, which does not necessarily require a hostage scenario, but which describes "strong emotional ties that develop between two persons where one person intermittently harasses, beats, threatens, abuses, or intimidates the other". In our current analysis the two persons are Belgium representing Europe and Congo representing Africa through traumatic bonding. It suggests that the bonding is the individual's response to trauma in becoming a victim. Identifying with the aggressor is one way that the ego defends itself. When a victim believes the same values as the aggressor, they cease to be perceived as a threat.

What is now called the Democratic Republic of Congo has clearly never recovered from King Leopold's legalised robbery enforced by violence, that has remained, more or less, the template by which Congo's contemporary rulers have governed ever since. If you brutalise someone for so long, they will end up identifying themselves with the brutaliser to heal the pain. This is what we see with people living in domestic abuse relationships. Meanwhile, Congo's soldiers have never moved away from the role allocated to them by Leopold II as a force to coerce, torment and rape the unarmed civilian population. From the Leopold's era, the major legacy left for the country was authoritarian rule and plunder. On the whole continent, perhaps no nation has had a harder time than the Congo in emerging from the shadow of its past.

These problems cascade down the generations, growing more complex over time. Traumatisation leads to feelings of deep anger and rage, this anger has no safe outlet as it can only be worked on and resolved in a safe environment, and is therefore stored in the body for later expression. This invariably occurs in an unstructured and explosive way.

What effect has our history had on our culture

and our soul? What are the impacts of generations of oppression of people? From early infancy through adulthood, trauma can alter the way we view ourselves, the world around us, and alter how we process information and the way we behave and respond to our environment.

In order to begin to understand the magnitude of King Leopold II's legacy on present-day Congolese people, it is important to examine the diagnostic characteristics of trauma. What are the effects of trauma on human beings? What does trauma look like? How does that trauma manifest itself?

If you chop someone's hand off, the victim would be severely traumatised. Someone passing by who saw the scene could also be traumatised. Some family member of the victim informed about the amputation may be intensely traumatized, while others very little. There might even be someone next to the victim who may not experience any symptoms of trauma whatsoever. This is because all human beings react to events differently. Bear in mind that thousands of children and adults had their right hands hacked off by Leopold's agents, to prove to their superiors that they had not been "wasting" their bullets on hunting for leisure. The huge rainforest of Congo teemed with wild rubber which was becoming the new gold, and Leopold pressed his agents for more of it. This is when the genocide reached its peak. Tapping wild rubber was a difficult affair, and Leopold's agents had to use brutal force to get the people of Congo to go into the forests and gather rubber for him. Any Congolese man, who resisted the order, saw his wife kidnapped and put in chains to force him to go and gather rubber. Or sometimes the wife was killed in revenge.

As more villages resisted the rubber order, Leopold's agents ordered the Force Publique army to raid the rebellious villages and kill the people. To make sure that the soldiers did not waste the bullets in hunting animals, their officers demanded to see the amputated right hand of every person they killed. As Hochschild puts it, "the standard proof was the right hand from a corpse, or occasionally not from a corpse. 'Sometimes', said one officer to a missionary, "soldiers shot a cartridge at an animal in hunting; they then cut off a hand from a living man". (King Leopold's Ghost: A Story of Greed, Terror and Heroism in Colonial Africa, by Adam Hochschild)

Lots of citizens are reported to be suffering from Post-Traumatic Stress disorder as a result of witnessing the oppression, the looting and the massive rape as a war weapon.

According to the definition (Psychological Bulletin, Vol 129(1), Jan 2003, 52-73.), some of the conditions which give rise to mental and /or emotional traumas that justify the diagnosis of Post-Traumatic Stress

Disorder are as follows:

1. A serious threat or harm to one's life or physical integrity
2. A threat of harm to one's close relative
3. A sudden destruction of one's home or community
4. Learning about a serious threat-to a relative or a close friend being tortured or killed
5. Stress is experienced with intense fear, terror and helplessness
6. Stress and disorder is considered to be more serious and will last longer when the stressor is of human design

It is important to note that the definition states that any one of the above stressors is enough to cause Post-Traumatic Stress Disorder, so what about the Congolese people who might have experienced all combined stressors?

From King Leopold's era, many people did not experience just one of the above stressors; rather many experienced all of them, and the great majority of Congolese were subjected to these traumatic experiences repeatedly. Taking this into consideration the fact that people were exposed to a lifetime of traumas, even though not everyone is affected by traumatic events, we could deduce without doubt that a considerable number of Congolese are likely to have suffered from post-traumatic stress disorder.

When we say post-traumatic syndrome, we are talking about behaviour, attitudes, beliefs, rituals, the kind of cultural determinants people were forced to pick up during the period of physical incarceration in chains. We recognise the tools that people had to use psychologically, socially and politically; the kind of personality and attitudes they had to form, the kind of relationships they had to build brother to brother, brother to sister, children to parents and parents to children. Many little nuances were developed to outwit the oppressor, to fool him, to mislead him, to survive to the next day.

The severe starvation, being worked to death, being beaten to death, females being raped before puberty, males being raped the same, and all these conditions of fear were inflicted on Congoleses indigenous.

In today's world, those who are diagnosed with post-traumatic stress disorder exhibit symptoms that may require clinical treatment inclusive of drug therapy. (Psychological Bulletin, Vol 129(1), Jan 2003, 52-73.) An individual may exhibit some of the symptoms for having had direct or indirect exposure to a single traumatic event.

What symptoms do you think those who

experienced a lifetime of oppression may exhibit, when taking into account the fact that people are still incarcerated, still enslaved by multinational mining companies, and people still prisoners of war?

The effects of the traumas have never been addressed, nor did the trauma cease for the Congolese people.

Since the capture and transport of the first Congolese slaves in 1400s when the Kongo Empire's first recorded contact with Europeans occurred, the indigenous people have had to deal with systematic efforts to destroy the bonds of relationships that held them together, as well as continuing efforts to have them believe themselves to be less than human. With free will at the core of being human, can you imagine what it must be like to have your will assaulted on a daily basis? Living in a society that tells you constantly, that everything about who you are, is wrong - the culture, the medicine, the finances, the spirituality and the economics?

Psychological control was cheaper to apply, therefore symbols and subliminal messages were aimed at the unconscious through text books, media and churches. From early infancy through adulthood, exposure to specific images have altered the way people viewed themselves and their world, and altered how they processed information and responded to their environment.

The colonisers forced everyone to convert to Christianity at the end of a blade or through the barrel of a gun. They were forced to worship a false god and his blonde haired, blue-eyed image. The colonisers robbed names, language, religion, culture, as well as customs and norms. They created institutions to keep people mentally enslaved and below average in society, and that still exist today in twenty-first century. Seeing a picture of white Jesus, or the white man as God, was easy to accept. As a result of centuries of slavery and oppression, most whites in their thoughts as well as actions believed themselves superior to blacks. Of greater import, too many Congolese unconsciously shared this belief till present day. This is not surprising, for as it is known, centuries of repetition and justification have gone into establishing such understanding.

Nationwide, Congolese people have continued to experience traumas similar to those of their past ancestors. Without intervention, these cognitive processes and behavioural responses can lead to deficiencies, performance problems, and problematic behaviour. Today only very few Congolese can afford to get clinical treatment for Post-Traumatic Stress Disorder at the Centre Neuro Psycho Pathologique (CNPP) in Kinshasa, which was created after 1954. (Dechef (G.) Chap. 17 Psychiatrie 3.3 Centre Neuro-Psycho-Pathologique pp.936-938 in P.G. Janssens, M. Kivits) .

It's common to hear people saying; "You know what, Europeans are tired of feeling guilty about what happened over a hundred years ago, so get over it." Or sometimes People ask, "How could the Congolese today possibly be affected by events that occurred so long ago? After all, Congo became independent half a century ago now!"

And the response would be, "If you're going to enjoy the wealth that was generated by evil, then you must take the curse that comes along with it." If you keep a well-known stolen good, then you are breaking the law. Therefore, even though you personally had nothing to do with it, because you have received stolen goods you must pay the price as well.

Also if you choose to fight and struggle to protect stolen goods and you defend them and organize your society and relationship around maintaining them, continuing to enhance them, then you must pay the price.

This is the reason why European countries live in terror; because descendants of the slave masters are defending their inheritance and way of life, but it doesn't matter how good they are or how liberal they are. The act does not end at the point of its occurrence; it continues to reverberate into the future and down across the generations on both sides of the oppressors and the victim. Why should we shy away from uncomfortable truths if we are all fighting on the same side of the battlefield! There are Belgians who just know what it is and actively work collaboratively to challenge racism and oppose Western imperialism, the rest are just liberal pretenders who can't even play catch up because they refuse to leave their privileged pretend world of make believe.

The struggles have not changed and the attitude of many descendants of colonisers generally remains the same. Martin Luther King Jr, said it best: "I have almost reached the regrettable conclusion that the Negroes great stumbling block in his stride towards freedom is not from the white citizens council or the ku klux klan but the white moderate who is more devoted to "order" than to justice; who prefers a negative peace which is the absence of tension to a positive peace which is the presence of justice... Shallow understanding from people of goodwill is more frustrating than absolute mis-understanding from people of ill-will." Martin Luther King, Jr. "Letter from the Birmingham Jail" April 16, 1963

What do people find so uncomfortable about engaging honestly in such a conversation and analysing and discussing the points and evidence being presented? The answer is extremely important because this is currently one of the biggest stumbling blocks in the Congo case. Belgium refuses to have a discussion on colonisation and its workings because it is afraid to look into its soul. It doesn't matter today which country directly experienced or participated in oppression. What does matter is that Congolese have experienced a legacy of trauma.

Most people raise their children upon how they were raised themselves. Parenting is one of an innumerable of skills that is passed down generation to generation. Parents moulded children's behaviour by inflicting fear to keep them alive and away from the trouble. For example, families frequently whipped children who attempted to stand their ground, to avoid them growing up stubborn. They are still doing it today, even parents living in European diaspora. This has been first introduced by Belgian coloniser as a way of subduing indigenous to force labour. It has been the result of lifetimes of abuse suffered through the generations.

Internet search results will paint odyssean portraits of thousands of American war veterans: restless and explosively violent, battling internal monsters, incapable of making the emotional return home years after they have left the physical combat zone. One in five American veterans who have served in Iraq or Afghanistan suffers from severe depression or post-traumatic stress disorder, a noxious bouquet of depression, hopelessness, panic attacks, psychosomatic pains, rage, and insomnia.

More active-duty troops had died of suicide than in combat. Mental disorder has become the signature injury of Washington's latest wars, which have turned the term and its acronym, PTSD, into household words in the United States.

But can an entire country have PTSD? Can invisible wounds bleed whole societies: failed states like the Democratic Republic of the Congo?

It is as important to address the effects of trauma on the psyche as to provide survivors with food, shelter, and physical health care. Extending behavioral help to the millions of people who raise their children, graze their livestock, tend their fields, and go to school every day against the macabre backdrop of mass rape, air raids, gunfights, minefields, torture, and political executions.

But how does one help heal a country that has been forged in millennia of almost incessant conflict? There is no such thing as a Marshall Plan for the mind.

We have to have social workers, psychiatrists, social psychologists, psychotherapists, psychiatric nurses.

Chapter 5: The King Leopold's subjects

So, what is the state of colonial children today? How are the impacts of past history visible? What are some of our behaviours that point to Post Traumatic Slave-colonial Syndrome? How are vacant esteem, ever-present anger and socialisation expressed in families and communities in the current millennium?

King Leopold developed a military dictatorship over a country 76 times the size of Belgium, with only a small number of white officials. Initially, he paid mercenaries, but in 1888 these were transformed into the soldiers. At its peak, there were 19,000 conscripted African soldiers and 420 European officers. Natives had to search out vines through inhospitable jungle. It was illegal to pay any indigenous people with money, so other more brutal forms of exhortation were employed. King Leopold spent hundreds of millions bribing editors and journalists, and even published his own articles under a false name to hide what was going on.

It is likely that Congolese behaviour in particular and Africans in general, as well as many others, is in large part related to trans-generational adaptations to survive the stifling effects associated with the past traumas of slavery raids, followed by King Leopold's private state exploitation, followed by Belgian colonisation, then the dictatorial regimes with their on-going oppressions. The Congolese bear the burdens of their ancestry to some degree. Years of slavery and colonisation certainly have had their impact. A portion of the impact has given rise to weakness that they have to understand, confront and deal with if they are to thrive. Another portion has provided us with great strengths upon which to build. In both regards, they all are colonial children.

The Congo experience is one of continual, violent attacks on the body, mind and spirit. The impact of centuries of oppression and plunder has left men, women and children traumatised throughout their lives and the violent attacks of the past era persist long after, to the present day. In the face of these wounds, they have adapted attitudes and behaviours to survive, and these adaptations continue to manifest today. Understanding how lifestyles are influenced by ancestors may open up new ways of addressing some of the most life –threatening problems.

Congolese people suffer from all of the social ills that plague society at large: sexual abuse, crime and moral decay, to name a few. It would be unwise to argue that every maladaptive manifestation of these ills is a result of Post Traumatic Slave-Colonial

Syndrome. Still, it would make sense to understand to what degree these and other problems of today directly relate to the oppression experience. What adaptive behaviours have been taken on that has led to harmful habits, habits that could be replaced with healthier ones? Some of the things that have come to be associated with Congolese culture are negative, demeaning and harmful, such as public displays of verbal aggression at parties or various other gatherings, eating food high in salt and fat content to achieve a curvy body. These and many others behaviours have come to be expected and are deemed acceptable.

The Congolese have unwittingly adopted habits and traditions that influence how they think, what they eat, what they believe about health and health care, how they manage interpersonal conflict and even how they behave sexually. The exploration of the past's influence on the present should form the basis for Post-Traumatic Stress Syndrome work and research. Who or what they perceive themselves to be is influenced first by those in the immediate environment, which confirms and reinforces their perspectives. Invariably parents, families and friends play a vital role in helping people form an image of them. Perhaps even more influential are all the sights and sounds one is exposed to on a daily basis. Families and communities act as role models for who to trust and who to fear, how to work, when and where to play and who to play with. They teach us about power: who has it, and how to live, love and survive without it.

The media has been a central vehicle for transmitting images to the masses. They control how images will be displayed as well as whom and what will be depicted. The media has been a powerful tool in shaping public perceptions of individuals and specific groups. They market what is acceptable and unacceptable to their consumers, guided by their owners. Schools, literature and mass media give an incomplete and often intentionally misleading view of who the Congolese are as a people.

When faced with racial prejudice and hypocrisy from a hostile dominant society, and when social inequality and powerlessness come to define ones lives, it can have a seriously adverse impact on what we come to believe ourselves to be. In the face of media's onslaught, those without the tools to defend themselves come to fulfil the roles the dominant culture tells them they must play. This can encourage self-degrading behaviours by which people exploit one another for material gain, distorted admiration and an appearance of power. One of the ways that Post-Traumatic Stress Syndrome is reflected today can be seen in the recurrence of such stereotypical behaviour. The Congolese music industry provides the viewer with its depiction of the Congolese stereotype complete with drama and wardrobe: "La Sape", sex and violence, nicknamed Congolese BMW: Beer, Music and Women. "Sapeurs," is a recent commercial Ad from Guinness and Abbott Mead Vickers BBDO (AMV BBDO), an advertising agency that works with brands to campaign by incorporating digital, social, experiential, print or broadcast media. The spot shines a light on The Congolese Society of Ambianceurs and Elegant Persons - known as Sapeurs. The name is derived from the French slang for dressing with class in abject poverty, brutalised in their everyday work.

The Sapeurs live by a moral code, where style and attitude counts over occupation or wealth. The ad follows the men as they shed their working clothes and transform themselves into polished, hat-wearing, cane-wielding style moguls - because, as the narrator says, "in life, you cannot always choose what you do, but you can always choose who you are." This stylish club, made up of blue-collar workers who dedicate their off time to colourful fashion, show off their bow ties, brightly coloured shirts, and pocket squares. They finish off their outfits with trilby hats and the obligatory pair of sharp sunglasses before heading to a dingy club where they start to sashay to the music.

When global marketers portray Africa, the goal is usually humour or pity. Rarely do brands treat

Africans as cultural equals; much less as inspirational role models. The spot is vanity, selfishness and materialism pitched as "inspirational "by Guinness. Because being well dressed and groomed, even in advert poverty is not testimony of civilization. Instead of spending thousands of money on themselves, these people should spend it on the community.

Congolese people drape themselves in gold and diamond necklaces and flaunt huge gaudy rings; they wear the most expensive designer shoes and clothes, as well as designer handbags, a picture of wealth. In the absence of true wealth, they use these to paint a picture of success to avoid the embarrassment they believe they will experience if the world knew their true circumstances. The façade wears thin in the face of living as you go daily, renting instead of owning, following instead of leading, and struggling just to keep the lights on.

People who believe themselves to have little worth, little power, little self-efficacy, will often do whatever they can do to don the trappings of power, even if it means acting out the demeaning roles society considers appropriate for them. Unconsciously fulfilling the roles of stereotypical hustler, pimp, thug or dangerous black man are just some of the ways one can be impacted by Post-Traumatic Syndrome. It is possible that the root of such role fulfilment is the issue of esteem. Lack of self-esteem is a critical piece of the puzzle in many other manifestations of the Syndrome. It plays a role in the tendency for self-sabotage, in the desire to shame one another, and in the propensity to compete against each other.

Why are there so many single Congolese women in the European diaspora and back home, raising children single handily? All of the groups that have held together started with strong family structures. They have long established the habit of family. When times get tough, they relied more on each other. Often under stress, they become even more unified.

Conversely, the Congolese history has been one of fragmentation. Oppressive conditions have rendered Congolese men impotent with regard to keeping their families together. Today, the ideal of having a working male head of household earning a more than adequate income, and a stay at home mom who spends her days raising the children has become an unattainable luxury. Falling short of what was never attainable, Congolese men and women punish one another for not living up to the elaborately constructed fantasy.

It is not surprising, after decades of being depicted as ineffectual and inferior, that some might begin to believe that failure is inevitable. It is the expectation of failure that stops many youths from seeking education. It is this same expectation that can stop hard working adults from seeking promotions and advancing their careers. Being told you are inferior for hundreds of years can have lasting psychological impacts, impacts that are passed from parent to child, to grandchild, to great grandchild. We know family traditions are passed down through generations.

The perpetual drama of finding ways to escape the shame is the result for people who have been robbed of any real knowledge of who they are and where they came from. It is a result of people who have no understanding of how they arrived at where they are now and who are unaware of how their past has predestined their present. People allow clothes, accessories, cars and all manner of material possessions to define their worth.

There seems to be a strange tendency amongst many Congolese to orchestrate and plot the demise of other Congolese, sometimes even friends and relatives. It is as though the achievement of family and friends, colleagues and acquaintances are seen as threat or an affront. We have been taught and socialised to believe that we are at the lowest level of progress and achievement, that we are lazy, untrustworthy and criminal. So it follows reason that when someone is promoted over another person, the person left behind experiences a profound sense of inferiority, as if there was a fear of being left behind by the very people who we embraced as in our equal status; people with whom we are bonded by inferiority. When a person is in a position of power, often as a manager, they will act as gatekeeper, charged with making sure those of his or her kind are kept in their place of inferiority.

Taking on the negative stereotype as their identity, developing low expectations for themselves, their families and communities; assuming that they will fail in most things that they set out to achieve; losing critical respect for themselves and thus diminishing others; perpetually trying to outrun the demon of shame by amassing material things in exchange for dignity; forgetting how to love themselves and each other: these are some of the ways the vacant esteem of Post Traumatic King Leopold II Syndrome is manifested today. These stand out as some of the most serious, persistent and deleterious expressions of the slave culture past.

The issue of respect is the most significant antecedent in the expression of violence. Socialisation occurs as families provide children with a historical and cultural map of the Congolese experience that describes how they have survived many adverse conditions beginning with year 1482 slavery. The children learn how the belief in God and extended family has served to strengthen and insulate them from the negative effects of oppression, racism and discrimination.

Being disrespected can be humiliating,

frustrating and belittling. It is natural for a person to get angry at even one slight. Blacks experience all manner of disrespect on a daily basis, at work, at the grocery store, at the mall, at school and even in the hospital. Perhaps most hurtful is when they are disrespected by their relatives. Historically, they have suffered the indignities of slavery, abuse and oppression for generations. When a person lacks a strong positive sense of themselves, every incident can be perceived to be a personal attack. Public humiliation or disrespect is a cardinal sin; it is also an unfortunate fact of life for too many.

Without sufficient self-esteem the idea of manhood is all there is left. *We have not been allowed to be men during oppression*, as Lumumba said in his independence speech 30 June 1960, and so the concept of manhood has yet to mature. A person is disrespected once too often at work so they blow up at their boss and lose their job. When they were younger, they were regularly disrespected by their teachers so they angrily decided education has no value. In the face of disrespect, whether real or perceived, one must find a more workable way of dealing with it. We have little control over how others will behave; however, we have a choice as to how we respond and a responsibility to exercise that choice in a way that is useful. The ways in which we choose to respond, influences the range of responses that our children come to believe are available to them. If we continue to be emotionally vulnerable to these acts of disrespect, we will relegate ourselves and our children to a life of victimisation. At the very least we need to learn how to overcome our initial feelings and reactions, and respond in a way that serves us.

Chapter 6: Generation Ingeta – The Democratic Republic of Congo today

Is the country ever going to really heal? We must face and resolve the unbearable feelings and memories we have long avoided, in order to heal the nation from psychological and emotional trauma. This process can involve processing trauma-related memories and feelings, building or rebuilding the ability to trust each other. How do we do this? We will be able to do this by completing our work with more thought, research and insight, and contribution from many within and outside of our community.

Trauma has disrupted the country's natural equilibrium, freezing it in a state of hyperarousal and fear. Its cycle of conflict has left faltering infrastructure, disrupted trade, and distorted markets, leaving millions in desperate poverty. In essence, all the country's vital systems have become stuck, making it one of the poorest countries on earth. However, the situation is not hopeless. That's why we need to have strong institutions, involve ourselves in social activism, deliver quality social services to those in need and provide mental, emotional and spiritual support and guidance for our own. Congolese entrepreneurs need to emerge to create corporations, establish philanthropic efforts, educate and support children, youths and adults. We need to set up programmes to provide not just relief but also a platform for forward progress, aiming to boost farm production, promote good governance and teach business skills.

One such strategy is to rebuild economic relationships between communities torn apart by long time oppression and violence. While there's no panacea to the DR Congo's myriad problems, only a sustained focus on long-term healing will break the cycle of conflict and poverty.

Understand why we are so low

We have been taught for a very long time to hold negative beliefs about our values and skills, we often self-sabotage our efforts or in some cases, we even cease trying at all. If we are to heal, one of the steps we must take is to ensure we build our own self-esteem as well as the self-esteem of our children. This might be a no easy task for our esteem has been pummelled by storms of slavery, exploitation, oppression and media marketing for so long. If we are to heal and become healthy we will do so by building upon our strengths. We will need to draw upon our inner fortitude, resilience and endurance. We will need to tap into our industriousness and creativity. Most of all we have to apply our spirituality and ability to love to the task before us. We have to reconnect with our own, and love our own African self and kind nature. Nature is not an external entity outside of ourselves; we are nature, governed by a supreme force, which is also a part of us.

Religions have mystified this force to the point where it no longer has tangible meaning. We refer to this force as the spirit, the energy that creates order in nature due to our high melanin content in our body and the ability of melanin to keep us more in tune with nature and vibration. Since nature is the creation of God, this means that anything that naturally creates or maintains order in nature is of the spirit of God. So to be of the spirit of God is to be in accordance to the natural cycles of nature. Hence, a spiritual person is one who is naturally obedient to the natural order. This is the reason why we are spiritual, loving and hopeful people. After all the work done to dominate, diminish and destroy us, after some of the vile and horrific abuses meant to break our spirit and will, we still have faith in God.

Telling our story

It is clear that surviving and struggling as Africans has often meant enduring tremendously demeaning and humiliating situations, remembered as shameful episodes not to be acknowledged or discussed. When a nation is injured, it becomes forced to remain relatively or completely inactive, or it becomes limited to a certain range of things and rehabilitation activities, either of which can profoundly affect the wellbeing of its people. Doctors say that when the brain produces less of the feel-good chemicals, the negative emotions surrounding any injury become harder to manage. In our communities, if men can't play the family leading role, they start experiencing social isolation. These negative emotional changes can result in real depression and people will find it hard to provide for their own families. Food and shelter will be in short supply. Communities that are heavily dependent on men as breadwinners will become vulnerable to starvation.

In an effort to move beyond the humiliation from past injustices, many of us have disassociated themselves from the indignities that we or our relatives experienced in the struggle to overcome slavery, systematic oppression and poverty. Our failure to pass along these accounts of our hereditary past becomes a detriment to ourselves and our children. Our children are not aware of how, and who, endured what, in order for them to exist today. They have little knowledge of the struggles and suffering experienced by their ancestors.

Far too many youths do not feel compelled to serve or give back in any way, even to the parents that have cared for them. They are detached from their history and ungrateful because they have been spared the details of their family's story. It is difficult, if not impossible, to instil a sense of pride and responsibility in children and youth when they remain ignorant about themselves.

We have a wealthy store of memories about struggle, perseverance and victory, replete with the usual host of characters that are included in such accounts. The Congolese are strong creative people, a seemingly infinitely resilient people. We have a long history of enduring and persevering through the severest of trials. Evidence of these qualities can be seen today through our struggle within our worldwide diaspora "ingeta". Through oppressive times and over decades we established a distinctive culture with new names, language, customs and behaviours. We have invented our own games, foods, music, art and fashions.

We are also forgiving people, and despite the relentless oppression, even from our neighbouring countries, there has been no organised retaliatory terrorism fuelled by hatred and rage, proving ourselves to be among the most magnanimous of people. We as people seem to have forgotten that this is who and what we are. We seem to have forgotten our own nobility. We have forgotten our own greatness; perhaps many of us have never known it. This is not surprising given all the time, money and energy spent over centuries to convince us to accept the degraded status imposed upon us.

Whatever the case, it is vital that we collectively regain this knowledge so we can take our rightful place in the world community. It is crucial that we come to understand ourselves and have that understanding infiltrate us to our very core, for such a deep understanding will make healing from our wounds that much more complete. We just need time to take pen to paper, to contemplate what's wrong, how or why it happened, and most importantly, the positive bit on how to prevent it from happening again. Writing can help release any exterior factors that are trying to control our inner world. We need to discover our unique gift as a nation and share it with others. Do we make the world a better place? From the music point of view, does our music inspire and ennoble people? Do we promote unconsciousness or awareness?

We spend too much time focusing on the negative and take the positive for granted. We are going to need to focus on what we do right and work to improve those things. The national football team has just won the African Cup without sophisticated sound financial organisation. We are used to praising people or other family members once they are dead as if to praise them in their presence would be improper. In the absence of voiced recognition and praise from people to whom we are accountable, it feels like they are not proud of what we are and carry a lifetime of self-doubt as to our worth. Healthy esteem will come from healthy and positives exchanges with the people in our lives on whom we depend for support and guidance. The nation needs to take time to consider all that went well previously, explore ways of making it even better, and plan on what will go well the next time.

However, it is extremely difficult for a nation to progress when the same hands that held the whip still hold almost all of the wealth and power. The only things we have the power to change are our thoughts and our actions as a nation. If we control our inner nation, our outer world will no longer affect or control us, or our emotions. No person or country has the power to make us feel a certain way, except for us. Our inner world is all we can really control. Our outside world can seem chaotic and crazy, but we have the choice to stay in control, positive and unaffected.

Other people or things around us may affect our mood, our day or even our entire life. The nature of how we feel may depend upon what happens. If people around us are positive and things are going right, we have an amazing day. If we are surrounded by people who are complaining, putting us down, or are negative, then we have a horrible day. The lack of control of these exterior factors in our life can become extremely challenging. We may feel like there is nothing we can do. Unfortunately, we cannot depend or wait for others to change their negative behaviour. It is important to get in touch with and in control of our inner homeland, so answers will be revealed to us. We hope to find that find that all the exterior factors will no longer matter, or affect us, just as Cuba did after fifty years of oppression. According to a Washington post paper, Cuba has a network of more than 12,000 facilities for medical care, which is characterized by accessibility to free services and prophylactic counselling. The sector has added almost 500,000 employees, located in a system that includes 11,492 clinics, 152 hospitals, 452 polyclinics, 126 dental clinics, 126 nursing homes, 142 maternity homes, 228 homes for the elderly and 13 institutes providing health care services, teaching and research. Cuba has one doctor per 143 inhabitants, one dentist per 878 inhabitants and one nurse for every 117. The entire healthcare workforce has been trained in the domestic health system. Cuba learnt, painfully, that the inner voice and confidence have more power than anything else.

Getting the support we need

A great many of the original traditions and customs were lost. What did survive were the tribal stories about the ancestors and the strong rhythmic songs. These vestiges of African culture were eventually melded into the new Christian theology and emerged as a form of worship that can truly be considered uniquely African. Religion has thrived on fear, because fear is the most efficient way of destroying both critical and creative thinking. If we are to become healthy, we need to return to the days of building and relying upon our spirit of community. Our deep commitment to God, spiritu700iy and religion should be one of our primary building blocks. Regardless of how poor a black community is, churches are always sustained and supported. People have been taught that as a group they should not trust one another. Sowing the seeds of distrust was an important tool employed by slave owners, and oppressors as a way of preventing uprisings.

Stress less

Any human being who has been exposed to stress early in their lives may find it difficult to manage and control their emotions as they get older, and this can result in limited learning ability in children. This is why, after decades of poverty and deprivation, one might expect the Congolese to be full of despair, yet there is energy among them that refuses to die. Popular Congolese music is everywhere, from the throbbing clubs of Kinshasa to the tinny transistor radios of people in remote streets. People still have hope, poise and dignity, and they still laugh a lot.

Readjusting goals and establishing Strong Leadership

Re-evaluating our political objectives can alleviate pressure during times of crisis by spreading awareness and consciousness among the people, by putting the bulk of our energy into healing and recovery, for when we are able to exercise power effectively again in our own country. So rather than focusing on regaining power quickly, we would allow ourselves to feel encouraged by progress, instead of discouraged by how far we have fallen from our previous goals. Our communities can no longer afford to have our collective voice silenced with a single shot, as with the Lumumba assassination. We can't look to a few individuals to provide guidance and direction. We must begin to look to ourselves for leadership. This is not to suggest that we ignore the leaders that we have, but rather to build communities of leaders so that the loss of one does not curtail our progress and growth.

We have to remain vigilant and questioning. We have to endeavour to keep ourselves informed and to keep our education current. We have to question the images we ourselves are portraying. We have to examine the sounds and pictures to which we expose ourselves. We have to filter what we hear on the news and strive to understand what is true. Racially socialising our children, teaching them about the strengths of their family and culture along with reality of discrimination and racism, gives them tools to emotionally and psychologically filter racist assaults against them personally and against Congolese people as a group. We should not send them into a racially charged battlefield unprepared, ignorant of the mental, emotional and social landmines that await them.

Young Congolese people coming out of college or university remain ignorant and uneducated, as they have not learnt the truths. Every child in school is taught that Adolf Hitler was the worst human being that ever lived, killing six million Jews while, on the other hand, they are taught that King Leopold II, who killed ten million people, is a hero and a philanthropist who deserves the erection of monuments to honour him. They don't mention that the modern building of the Brussels city was paid for with the blood of their Ancestors. This miseducation is designed to corrupt the Congolese sense of unity and cohesion, and to mould self-hatred. Hence, many Congolese behave as though they believe that Europeans are somehow better, that we are the deficient people that the Europeans say we are. This is one of the most insidious consequences of post-traumatic stress disorder.

Many of today's leaders display some of the inappropriate behaviour discussed earlier. Their failure leaves more than 70 million of Congolese in a leadership crisis. How can we reasonably explain, for example the fact that, Denis Sassou Nguesso, the head of state of Congo- Brazzaville spent four days in Carratraca, Málaga in Spain? Why, to thank the neighbours for the welcome he received, he distributed 12 € one by one to the almost 900 inhabitants of that village?

We need to address the corrupt leaders who are placed in positions of power or leadership and become so afraid of losing their position that they will sell out the support base that put them there. We have to stop supporting incompetent leaders, because in doing so we lose our credibility as a group. We need a community of leaders to expand our base of role models, show us paths to success, guide and mentor us. We need social activist leadership to keep us on the path to community growth. We need leaders in education to expand the role and capacities of our educational institutions. We also need leaders who will return to our communities and aid in the creation of Congolese-owned businesses. If we are to develop a community of leaders, we must educate them to remain conscious and respectful of their connection to those they would lead.

Therefore, we need to act as role models of the behaviour we want our children to exhibit. We must model those attributes we want them to learn. Currently, there is a worrying culture whereby people are actively discouraged from taking a role and interest in politics. This is not healthy for the future of our democracy and we must therefore, tackle the crisis head on in order to reverse this culture. The qualifications and competences of people are the central raw material and, as such, crucial factors in international competition. They are the key to every country's future.

In order for people to fulfil their roles as citizens, now and in the future, we must allow them to discuss and debate in school. We must encourage and teach the youth to take an active role in politics, learn about political systems, class struggles, revolutionary processes, and to work as a collective.

Seeing and modelling the opportunity

We have failed to guide and to protect, to teach morals and principle, to teach our African history, to uphold community, to uphold traditions, to build upon foundations laid, to set up economic structures, to support our own businesses, to trust each other, to greet each other, to show love to each other. At this point in the healing process, we're getting stronger, and something exciting could start happening: our broken infrastructure system or dislocated educational system or economy may suddenly feel like an opportunity. True and lasting healing can be attained only with people who are free, equal, educated and have dignified social relations. Education as part of the arsenal is a precondition for winning the struggle against domination; preparing people to seize power themselves, to have the ability to get things done despite the resistance and opposition of others. To be empowered is to be set free. The best cultural education can change our sense of the wider world around us, opening up possibilities for our future that may have previously seemed outside of our grasp. Specific cultural education such as art and design, dance, drama, and music has direct educational benefits, enabling people to gain valuable knowledge and skills that stay with them for the rest of their lives.

Getting back on our feet

Writing about specific experiences, talking about nothing other than good testimonies and experiences, and finding new ways to strengthen our skills all help us to heal. Ingeta is the word symbolising revolution as a search for national identity. To judge the intellectual capacity and commitment of a group of people, we must follow the evolution of the mass as a whole. Africans have been able to organise states, to establish and maintain study centres such as Timbuktu, to produce statesmen like King Nzinga Nkuvu, and conquerors such as Ngongo Lutete. In addition, they have produced scientists and scholars who have succeeded without the help of any language dictionary to form idioms whose flexibility, richness and precision are to the astonishment of all those studying them, a fully sustainable system of writing. Our people do not deserve to be treated as inferior. We are just a race that has been programmed not to rely on itself to progress.

CONCLUSION

We aim to expose people to the politico-historical events that have led to present social problems and structural inequalities that continue to have a negative impact on the Congolese community today. To enable students to develop a knowledge base and a critical awareness of the problems that specifically affects the Congolese in practice and policy as well as the development of techniques useful for practice. To provide practical tools that will inform individuals, families, groups, organizations and communities throughout the change process.

Current society makes people think in straight lines instead of seeing the wider picture; we need people who can make connections in order to promote the full development of the personality, talents, and mental and physical capabilities of each individual. We can start rebuilding by public education about trauma, depression and anxiety from our history. We should teach our schoolchildren daily healing rituals with positive beliefs about their ability and worth; then they will be more likely to achieve the results they are after. Creating value on a daily basis will provide strong, incontrovertible evidence of our efficacy and worth.

King Leopold II's takeover of Congo territory set in motion a brutal colonial regime that revealed the core dangers of the racist imperial cynical scepticism when practiced within a society with over 30 million people that was a personal property of a single individual. He disguised its imperial and colonial ambitions and intentions under scientific and philanthropic designs.

King Leopold II employed the colonial concept of terres vacantes (vacant/empty lands). This was a common strategy to justify land expropriations. His next step was to demarcate Congolese territory into two zones. Of these, the Free Trade Zone was to be the domain of Europeans. It was a domain of free entrepreneurial enterprises, private ownership of land, and freedom to buy 10-15 year monopoly leases on anything of value including ivory and rubber. The second zone was the "Domaine Privé" (the exclusive private property of the state, embodied in the person of King Leopold II). The Domaine Privé comprised almost two-thirds of the Congo. There was no designated place for indigenous African people except through regroupment into ethnicised labour, providing colonial formations supervised by defeated native authorities

Western freedoms and their way of life are shored up by Congo's resources, estimated to be 24 trillion US dollars, equivalent to the GDP of

Europe and the United States combined. Politically Congo is kept in a hostile environment, at an infantile level of development that suit the rulers and multinationals companies who are making sure that there is no home-grown elite to run the country. We courageously created the independence movement that put Belgium to shame before the world but due to the syndrome, the independence movement desired to take the coloniser place, and chose to be in partnership with it, a part of the oppressive machine. Helping the oppressor design a better exploitation system, we started imitating the coloniser, and we called ourselves "evolués" or "civilised". The "evolués" then became the role model for the education of our children.

The current violence tormenting the Democratic Republic of Congo (DRC) has its roots in these Leopoldian colonial policies. In the first place, King Leopold II introduced the culture where a leader was able to exercise military, economic, and political control over a subnational territory within a sovereign state due to their ability to mobilize loyal armed forces that subsisted on terrorization of the population.

The present day violence in the eastern part of the DRC is to be traced to the time of dictatorship of King Leopold II, that created homelands supervised by 'native black' authorities. The reorganization of the indigenous population into rigid homelands enabled easy colonial organization for recruitment of cheap and forced labour. This colonial arrangement inaugurated rigid 'ethnic' identities as the basis for recruitment. Recruitment to mines, plantations, civil service, and the army became based on tribal identity. With a long term twofold impacts, this regroupment of identities meant first, that Congolese nationalism emerged as a deeply ethnicised phenomenon. Secondly, the question of who was indigenous to particular areas metamorphosed into the present day question of citizenship, a question which is generating violence in the eastern part of the DRC bordering Uganda, Rwanda and Burundi. Since the time of Leopold II, those who succeeded him - including Patrice Lumumba, Mobutu Sese Seko, Laurent Kabila and Joseph Kabila - have not managed to deal effectively with the questions of citizenship and identity in the DRC. Colonialism invented indigene versus non-indigene dichotomies that have continued to breed intra-and inter-communal violence in the DRC. In short, the violence that is currently haunting the DRC is intermingled with the question of citizenship whose roots are traceable to the time of Leopold II.

However, now times have changed, we are still behaving out of habit just because that the way we grew up doing things. We haven't passed on our history; people have forgotten why we got in this situation in the first place, and what purpose it served. We are trying to suppress ingeta, the Congolese diaspora revolutionary movement, to please the oppressors because it is antagonising for them. Those habits, behaviour, attitudes and beliefs are still carrying on today. We have to understand our last three to four generation's history. We need to remember our pain, we need to feel the pain and anger of our ancestors whose hands were chopped off for rubber, we need to remember the screams of our raped women, and we need to feel all that pain to get the motivation to change things around for the revolution. We need to know why we are struggling. No one should deny our ancestors' heritage. We have to keep in mind as we reclaim our African ancestry and the rich legacy and traditions which are phenomenal and unmatched by any of our fellow humans that, many of our people remain in a mental state of slavery.

We need to study our history and create a new one for ourselves. We need to create a new social language and model to motivate our children. We need to appeal to all men and women to reclaim what we know was our central and predominant faith before the invasion as a therapeutic intervention to heal and relieve our minds, our bodies and our souls from this disease known as Post King Leopold

Traumatic Syndrome. Somebody has to bring a stop to this.

Power is the ability to get things done despite the resistance and opposition of others. Politics is about power to decide who has food, income, education, shelter, and health care. Economics is the production, distribution and consumption of goods and wealth. We must learn alternative ways in which to combine power, politics and economics to create wealth and wellbeing by capitalising human resources. Firstly, wealth can be created as the fruit of any labour that is stored and used to satisfy human desires and needs; or acquired through redistribution, through inheritance, reparations or profit from someone else's labour. Much of the wealth that we need is right before our eyes. If we aggregate, we can see it. If we work together, we can acquire it or create it.

We must stop the brain drain that is taking the best and talented people out of our communities. We need to send our children off to get a good education so they can use their training and skills to take care of their own group first. Our schools, churches, and organisations must join in the effort to instil the desire for creating employment and wealth-building opportunities within our own communities to end or reverse the brain drain. Organisations can help reduce the brain drain by fostering and promoting public policy incentives and practices that encourage and provide financial and tax incentives specifically to inner city local companies that employ local people. School is where we should teach skills like research, critical thinking, logic, collaboration and presentation. Facts will be absorbed as a part of that process and so should only rarely require explicitly teaching. Let them find their own passion and they will seek out the education they need to achieve it.

True democracy can only be attained with people who are free, equal, educated and have dignified and productive jobs. Education is also part of the arsenal of revolution as a search for national identity. Educating the poor is a precondition for winning the struggle against imperialist domination, preparing them to seize power themselves. To be educated is to be free. This is why we suggesting for the Economic development of the Congo three orientations to Education:

> Education as a culture with basic literacy classes.

The best cultural education can change a person's sense of the wider world around them, opening up possibilities for their future that may have previously seemed outside of their grasp. People no longer need the model that assumes there are a thousand obedient worker bees for each queen bee. People are being educated for the demands of today's society. This society makes people to think in straight lines instead of seeing the wider picture; we need people who can make connections, unexpected connections. The aim of education must be to promote the full development of the personality, talents, and mental and physical capabilities of each individual. What's more, the study of specific cultural education subjects such as art and design, dance, drama, film studies and music has direct educational benefits; enabling people to gain valuable knowledge and skills that stay with them for the rest of their lives.

➤ Political education:

Currently, there is a worrying culture whereby people are actively discouraged from taking a role and interest in politics. This is not healthy for the future of our democracy and we must therefore, tackle the crisis head on in order to reverse this. In order for people to fulfil their roles as citizens, now and in the future, we must allow them to discuss and debate in school. We must encourage and teach the youth to take an active role in politics, learn about imperialism, class struggles, revolutionary processes, and work as a collective. The qualifications and competences of people should become the central "raw material" and, as such, crucial factors of international competition. They are the key to every country's future.

➤   Production education:

Learning of the processes and methods used to transform tangible inputs (raw materials, semi-finished goods, subassemblies) and intangible inputs (ideas, information, knowledge) into goods or services. Resources are used in this process to create an output that is suitable for use or has exchange value. Accountancy, technical training, specialization and cultivating the necessary toughness required to manage complex industries.

Churches in Congo helped to establish a foundation that supported exploitation. They were established to keep people pacified and under control. But like those early independent ministers who used their churches to help their people escape exploitation, we call on those religious organisations to be agents of change to empower Congolese today. Many religions are represented and there is a role for all of them .They can work together on common ground to establish and strengthen communities. In doing so we strengthen ourselves and the religion to which we belong. The many roles for churches presented here are suggestions based upon our need, history and analysis of issues. Church leaders have to work together to fine tune these suggestions and shape them so that they are practical. Some are functions in which the churches should work cooperatively with other institutions. Not all churches will venture from their comfortable niches to work toward this vision, but there will be many rewards for those who do.

It is from the impacts of past assaults that we must heal, and it is from the threats of continuing assaults that we must learn to defend ourselves, our families and our communities. Only through a greater understanding of conflicts and the myriad of mental health problems that arise from them can coherent and effective strategies for dealing with such problems be developed. To facilitate the Spiritual evolution of the individual, to awaken the Spirit, to facilitate a paradigm shift and to bring in a new brighter age in which everyone can live life, facilitate relationships and do business in a win-win manner.

Life has a purpose and that purpose is to grow, learn, evolve, and overcome our limitations and to see through our illusions. Life is about developing power, knowledge and wisdom and the moral compass to use them constructively - to the benefit of self, others and the greater collective. It is about empowering ourselves by discarding our own illusions and limitations, re-connecting to the Source and enhancing our energetic relationship to ourselves and our world.

Sources and References

1.   Kingdom of North Sudan, on page 20.
Slate the online magazine wrote on 14 july 2014, a American man plant flags in remote sudanes regions so that his daughter can be a princess, by Joshua keating

2.   After the murder of a black person, whites often kept souvenirs, page 26
Encyclopaedia of the Harlem Renaissance, By Aberjhani, Sandra L. West page 207
Birth Of A Nation-Hood: Gaze, Script, and Spectacle in the O J Simpson Case By Toni Morrison.

3.   Dr. Amos citation on page 32
Dr. Amos N. Wilson (February 23, 1941 – January 14, 1995) was an African-American theoretical psychologist, social theorist, Pan-African thinker, scholar and author.

4.   Twenty years ago, page 6
In 1976, a Belgian man went to Burundi in Africa.

5.   *"Monkey, eat your banana!" page 42,*
On October 26 Angers Magazine Info in France, delivered the proof in video revealing insults that accompanied Angers protest to the reception of the Minister of Justice Taubira. The video was made by Mickey Kuyo on October 25th, 2013 - It clearly shows one of the children brandishing the banana skin for the attention of the Garde des Sceaux Minister.

6.   *An ergastulum page 45,*
Roman building used to hold in chains dangerous slaves, or to punish other slaves. The ergastulum was usually subsurface, built as a deep, roofed pit - large enough to allow the slaves to work within it and containing narrow spaces in which they slept.

7.   *Fellah, page 45*
A peasant in Arab countries

8.   *Inhuman medical studies and experiments, page 63*
Medical Apartheid: The Dark History of Medical Experimentation
on Black Americans from Colonial Times to the Present, Harriet A.
Washington, Knopf Doubleday Publishing Group, 8 Jan 2008

9.   *These accusations are far from paranoid*, page 63
Debating AZT : Mbeki and the AIDS Drug Controversy, by Antho-
ny Brink. 1999.On 28 October 1999, after reading an early draft of
High Court advocate Anthony Brink's book, South African President
Thabo Mbeki ordered an inquiry into the safety of the AIDS drug
AZT. This book is only available in a .pdf file which you can open
and then save on your computer.

10.   *Speech Delivered by King Leopold II, page 65, 66, 67.*
Speech Delivered by King Leopold II to the Missionaries Journey-
ing to the Congo in 1883. Translated from French by Prince Asiel
Center for International Studies, USA

11.   *Page 90*
Black Out: What Has Happened to the Black Models? Ebony - Vol.
63, No. 11 - Magazine
The fashion cult cut from a different cloth Errol Barnett, CNN.

12.   *La Sape, page 91*
BBC News Magazine: Congo sapeurs: Is the Guinness ad true to
life? Ad Breakdown. The Magazine's review of advertising

Bibliography

Ascherson, N. *The King Incorporated*, London: Granta Books. P310, 1999

Morel E.D. *History of the Congo Reform Movement*, Oxford University Press, 1968

Reeves, J. S. *The International Beginnings of the Congo Free State.* Baltimore: The Johns Hopkins Press. p. 32, 1894

F. Cattier, *Droit et Administration de l'*État *Indépendant du Congo* . Brussels, 1898 p.134

Ewans, M. *European Atrocity, African Catastrophe: Leopold II, the Congo Free State and its Aftermath*, London 2002, Routledge Curzon. p.114.

The Congo: A Report of the Mission of Enquiry Appointed by the Free State Government 1905

Nelson, S. H. (1994) *Colonialism in the Congo Basin 1880-1914.* Ohio University Center for International Studies: Ohio, 1994, p. 92.

Hochschild, A, King *Leopold's Ghost: A Story of Greed, Terror and Heroism in Colonial Africa.* Macmillan: London, 1998 p.123

Arthur A. Slatkin. *The Stockholm syndrome and Situational Factors Related to Its' Development.* University of Louisville, 1997, 308 pages

Apel, Dora. *Imagery of Lynching: Black Men, White Women, and the Mob.* Rutgers University Press.2004, 304 pages.

Armstrong, Julie Buckner. *Mary Turner and the Memory of Lynching.* University of Georgia, Press. 2011

Finkelman, P. *Encyclopedia of African American history, 1896 to the present: from the age of segregation to the twenty-first century.* New York: Oxford University Press, 2009.

DuRocher, Kristina. *Raising Racists: The Socialization of White Children in the Jim Crow South.* University Press of Kentucky, 2011 -248 Pages

Dembour, Marie- Bénédicte . *Recalling the Belgian Congo: Conversations and Introspection.* Berghahn Books, 2000 256 pagesDembour, Marie- Bénédicte. *The Memory of Colonialism: Meetings with Former Colonial Officers of the Belgian Congo.* University of

Oxford, 1993 263 pages

Frankema E. and Buelens F. *Colonial Exploitation and Economic Development: The Belgian Congo and the Netherlands Indies Compared.* Routledge explorations in economic history, 2013Burrows, Guy. *The Curse of Central Africa.*

R. A. Everett & Company, Limited, 1903,276 pMartin Mike, Baker Chloe and Hatch-Barnwell Charlie. *Crossing the Congo: Over Land and Water in a Hard Place.* Oxford University Press, 2016

Butcher Tim. *Blood River: A Journey to Africa's Broken Heart.* Vintage, 2008, 363 pages

TRICORN
BOOKS